History Afield

History Afield

Stories from the Golden Age of Wisconsin Sporting Life

Robert C. Willging

Wisconsin Historical Society Press

Published by the Wisconsin Historical Society Press
Publishers since 1855

© 2011 by the State Historical Society of Wisconsin

wisconsin history.org

Photographs identified with WHi or WHS are from the Society's collections; address requests to reproduce these photos to the Visual Materials Archivist at the Wisconsin Historical Society, 816 State Street, Madison, WI 53706.

Printed in Wisconsin, U.S.A.
Designed by Brad Norr Design

15 14 13 12 11   1 2 3 4 5

Library of Congress Cataloging-in-Publication Data
Willging, Robert C.
  History afield : stories from the golden age of Wisconsin sporting life / Robert C. Willging.
    p. cm.
  Includes bibliographical references and index.
  ISBN 978-0-87020-429-6 (hardcover : alk. paper) 1. Sports—Wisconsin—History. 2. Recreation—Wisconsin—History. I. Title.
  GV584.W6W55 2011
  796.09775—dc22
                    2010043583

Cover: Hunting Prairie Chickens, WHi Image ID 10150
Frontispiece: Craftsman with handmade lodge sign, courtesy of the author
Back Cover: Gypsy Rose Lee Fishing, WHi Image ID 2110

∞ The paper used in this publication meets the minimum requirements of the American National Standard for Information Sciences—Permanence of Paper for Printed Library Materials, ANSI Z39.48–1992.

For Mom and Dad

Boats awaiting vacationing fishermen WHi Image ID 39612

Contents

Louis Spray with mounted musky Courtesy of the author

Acknowledgments

I began writing about Wisconsin's outdoor and sporting history for my "History Afield" column in the year 2000, and the stories in this book span a decade of work. Through the years I have met many wonderful people who were willing to share their knowledge and excitement about Wisconsin history—and many times their own personal stories and photos— with me.

I am particularly grateful for the support and assistance provided by Mitch Mode, Rhinelander; Joel and Janet McClure, Phelps; Leon Pastika, Hayward; Wendy Robinson, Rhinelander, and her mom Doris Goldsworthy, Three Lakes; Tim and Prudence Ross, Hayward; Mike Sheldon, Antigo; Rich Devlin, Enterprise; Joy Vancos, Rhinelander; Jim Montgomery, Rhinelander; Ken Schels, Eagle River; Neal Lendved, Green Bay; Ducky and Laurel Reed, Oconto; and Sue and Al Rosenquist, Hayward.

Several people I interviewed for the column are now deceased. The very reason they had so much to share was that they had lived long lives full of memorable experiences. Those who have passed on have left an indelible mark in my mind. They include John and Mary Barth, Pardeeville; Vern Frechette, Washburn; Marv Kaukl, Poynette; John Mistely, Enterprise; Vernon "Duke" and Dorothy Montgomery, Rhinelander; and sisters Shirley Sleight and Dorothy Uthe, Mercer.

The expertise and support of the Wisconsin Historical Society Press, including John Motoviloff, Laura Kearney, Kathy Borkowski, Kate Thompson, Rachel Cordasco, and the talented production staff, contributed greatly to the development and successful completion of this book.

There is always a quiet corner to write at the Rhinelander District Library, and I'd like to thank the staff there. A rare operating Andrew Carnegie library—

although it has expanded from the original 1903 Carnegie grant portion—
Rhinelander's free library is an ongoing example of the enormous importance of
public libraries to a democracy.

Introduction

I crossed paths with the old man at a logging museum in Hayward, a small town in Sawyer County situated on the banks of the Namekagon River, one summer afternoon in 1982. I was in my early twenties and between my junior and senior years at UW–Stevens Point (UWSP), where I was studying wildlife biology. I remember thinking the old man was about the same age as my grandparents—my primary reference point for very old people at the time—who were in their eighties. He was stooped from what I imagined was a life of hard labor, and suspenders held up his pants.

I had been to this logging museum once or twice before that summer as Hayward was a grocery shopping destination for me and several other college students who were working as summer volunteers for the Chequamegon National Forest (now part of the Chequamegon-Nicolet National Forest), stationed at a relatively remote Forest Service camp north of the tiny community of Clam Lake. Volunteering was about the only way to get experience to put on job applications and résumés in the midst of a poor economy and equally poor job prospects in the field of natural resources management.

I liked the museum and its collection of turn-of-the-century north Wisconsin logging artifacts. I was just beginning to become aware of north Wisconsin's big pine logging era history. While tramping the woods of the Chequamegon I often came across silver gray skeletons of what had once been enormous pine stumps— the only remnants of the old-growth trees that had been felled by loggers working two-man crosscut saws. After nearly a century most were no more than the outer wood, the center having decayed, but their shape and great diameter (perhaps four to five feet across) were obvious. In the open hardwood forest that had replaced the pine stand I could see wide spacing of the stumps and imagine the trees that had once stretched 150 feet or more toward the sky. I had the same feeling at the museum—the feeling of being connected to the past through the artifacts that have survived.

Through time I've lost the detailed memories of the man—his name, where he was from, why he was there at the museum on that day. What I do remember is that he had stories to tell, and he wasn't shy about telling them to me. He latched onto me as I was walking through the outdoor area of the museum, where the ragtag collection of old logging equipment could be found. He not only told me about each item—what it was called and what it did—he had a story attached to each one, stories that usually involved himself or someone he knew. He told me things I really didn't want to know as well, such as the very detailed description of how he developed a groin "rupture" or hernia while working on a farm.

What I didn't fully realize or appreciate at the time was that I was lucky enough to have an old-timer—someone who may at sometime in his life have been a white pine logger, or at least certainly was well acquainted with turn-of-the-century loggers—giving me a private, guided tour of a logging museum. Thinking back on that experience today, I regret not having asked the man more questions or better understanding the opportunity to learn about northwoods Wisconsin history from a person who had lived it.

A few years later, after graduating from UWSP and bouncing around the country from one short-term job to another—always trying to get that field experience that would help me land a permanent job—I found myself back in school, this time graduate school at New Mexico State University (NMSU). My graduate fieldwork took me to a remote national forest in the very corner, the boot heel, of southwest New Mexico, along the Arizona and Mexican borders. The Peloncillo Mountains, a narrow desert range that straddles the Arizona–New Mexico border and stretches north from the Mexican border up to the Gila River, were my study area as I researched the Gould's turkey, the largest of the five subspecies of wild turkey found in North America, and it was here that I ran into another old-timer.

Vernon lived in a small trailer on a cattle ranch located near the mountain pass where the only travel route, a dusty gravel road known as the Geronimo Trail, dropped down into Arizona. Like the man in Wisconsin, Vernon was in his eighties and also had tales to share and was happy to share them with me.

Vernon, as I recall, had retired long ago from a job in the city and was working as a hired hand on the ranch, mostly in return for a place to park his trailer. He seemed to have plenty of time for his greatest passion, exploring the mountains with his pack of blue heeler dogs. More than once the loyal and feisty heelers had protected Vernon from rattlesnakes and attacks from javelinas (the collared peccary, which possesses razor-sharp tusks).

Vernon's trailer was filled with the prizes he had discovered on his explorations, and he would describe each item's historical significance—a little glass bottle that he told me had once held grape juice for the U.S. Army soldiers on the trail of Geronimo (Geronimo had surrendered to the army in Skeleton Canyon, just to the north). Grape juice was given to soldiers to prevent scurvy. He also had found a lever-action rifle dating back to the 1800s wedged in the crook of a tree, as well as rifle cartridges, cannonballs, military belt buckles, and some pottery and silverware from early settlers. The little trailer was like a museum of the Peloncillo Mountains. Once again I was lucky to have an old-timer teach me a little history.

It wasn't until many years later and after I moved to Rhinelander that I was able to put the great resources of an old-timer to pen and paper. In 2000 I began writing for *Wisconsin Outdoor News* (*WON*), a biweekly hunting and fishing newspaper, when my interest in writing about outdoors and sporting history brought me together with *WON* editor Dean Bortz. My first major contribution to *WON* was a decade-by-decade series on the history of deer hunting in Wisconsin from 1900 through the end of the century (the genesis of my first book, *On the Hunt: The History of Deer Hunting in Wisconsin*).

As I stared at microfilms of old newspapers at the Rhinelander District Library one evening while researching deer hunting history, a middle-aged man, Rich Devlin, struck up a conversation. As we discussed what I was doing he told me the story of his grandfather, and what a story it was. Edward Keeler was the son of the first white settlers of the area that would become the Town of Enterprise, one of the Oneida County townships south of Rhinelander. Keeler was an interesting man, a prominent citizen in the township—he farmed in the summer, as well as operating a large boat on Pelican Lake (which delivered tourists and supplies to the resorts on the lake), the largest natural lake in Oneida County. In the winter he enjoyed fur trapping.

What made Keeler's story unique was that he met a strange and untimely death, shot in the woods near his trapping cabin, the murderer never found. This was early 1930s northern Wisconsin, where moonshiners and gangsters were not uncommon. Devlin encouraged me to write about the incident and suggested I talk to a man named John Mistely, who lived near Pelican Lake. Mistely had not only been friends with Edward Keeler, he remembered firsthand the details of when Keeler went missing—Mistely had participated in the search party that eventually found his body.

I met Mistely at his rural home, and although he was ninety-four years old, his mind was sharp and he delighted in discussing the nearly seventy-year-old crime with me. This time I realized right off the bat how amazing it was to hear about this unique tidbit of northwoods history from someone who was actually there. Through this old-timer I was able to make a direct connection to early Oneida County history.

Edward Keeler's story appeared in *Wisconsin Outdoor News* January 7, 2000, and is a part of this book. The Keeler story and the deer hunting history pieces led to a regular column in *WON* that focused on Wisconsin's outdoors and sporting history. I called the column "History Afield." In the introduction to the first official "History Afield" column, I wrote:

There is a great importance for a society to know its history. Without learning history we run the risk of believing that what is now has always been. We run the risk of believing that the world has always had cable television and cell phones and endless fast food restaurants. I believe the importance of hunting, fishing, and trapping history is even more important as we rocket into the new century. The pioneers that settled Wisconsin, the ancient Indian hunters, the old guides, and the long past woodsmen didn't leave much of a written record, and each new generation becomes further isolated from the land and our incredible sporting heritage. It is important to remind ourselves that people were once satisfied with simple things, and outdoor pursuits—hunting, fishing, trapping—were important components of the quality of life. The decisions made by generations long ago have given us the world we live in today—the public lands we enjoy, the ideas of scientific wildlife management, the freedom to possess firearms in pursuit of game. Through this column I plan to revisit the events, people, and places of a Wisconsin that used to be.

Introduction

As I began accumulating stories for the column I quickly began to realize what an incredible sporting and outdoors history Wisconsin lays claim to. And just as quickly I began to realize how relatively little of it is recorded for future generations to learn from and enjoy. In addition, what is out there isn't always easily accessible for the average person, such as self-published local books that might exist in only one library or material archived at a local museum (many of which in small towns, particularly those in northern Wisconsin, are open only part of the year).

To be sure, some great outdoor writing from years past has preserved portions of the way Wisconsin sporting life once was, and some of this is very accessible. The most prominent examples are several published collections of "Old Duck Hunters Association" stories by Gordon MacQuarrie.

MacQuarrie was one of Wisconsin's most prolific and best-known outdoor writers of the 1930s, '40s, and early '50s, and he served as the *Milwaukee Journal*'s first outdoors editor, accepting the job in 1935. Keith Crowley in *Gordon MacQuarrie: The Story of an Old Duck Hunter* wrote: "When MacQuarrie began at the *Journal* on April 19 he didn't have an official title, but he was in effect becoming the first full-time professional outdoor writer in the nation."

Although MacQuarrie wrote hundreds of articles about a wide variety of sporting subjects for both the *Journal* and the big national outdoor magazines, it is his nearly sixty "Old Duck Hunters" stories that hold the greatest significance for Wisconsin-based readers and Wisconsin history. MacQuarrie created the fictional organization The Old Duck Hunters Association, Inc. (the "Inc." was short for incorrigible) as a vehicle to present the reader the very best he had to offer. In the ODHA stories he brilliantly pulled together his love of his favorite places on earth (most notably northwest Wisconsin, where the Bois Brule River and the Eau Claire Chain of Lakes could be found), his favorite sporting activities (trout fishing the Brule and waterfowl hunting the area's lakes and bays and potholes), and an admiration for the people who lived in his favorite places.

MacQuarrie completely understood the importance of the old-timer, and his ODHA stories were populated by a host of them, foremost his father-in-law, Al Peck, but also a contingent of other characters whom MacQuarrie skillfully used to tell the stories. After reading a few ODHA stories one cannot help but be transported back to MacQuarrie's time—you begin to know exactly what it felt like to be fishing the Brule River on a springtime opening day or late-season hunting for bluebills on a storm-tossed lake. I don't know if MacQuarrie ever had posterity in mind while writing an ODHA story, but nevertheless he documented a sporting way of life that we will never see again.

The publication dates for the stories in *History Afield* span about a decade. The columns I wrote that focused on deer hunting history ended up in some form, usually the theme of a sidebar, in *On the Hunt*. This book, which includes one previously unpublished piece, is a collection of the best of those that did not appear in *On the Hunt*.

These pieces range far and wide—from the Indians and voyageurs who accessed the Mississippi River via the Fox-Wisconsin waterway and portage to the resort men who lured tourists to the northwoods through the promise of sometimes-rustic, sometimes-elegant accommodations and a chance to forget about the world for a week or two; from remembrances of hunting with live duck decoys to the little-known connection between New York's Cornell University and the old-growth white pine forest of Wisconsin's Chippewa River watershed; from sporting goods stores with rich histories of providing the gear for sports enthusiasts as well as a gathering place to show off a trophy musky or blue-ribbon whitetail to the presidents, Cal and Ike, who visited Wisconsin to pursue a sporting life, if only for a little while.

Documenting Wisconsin's incredibly rich sporting heritage—keeping these stories close at hand, remembering them, rereading them—reminds us that simple outdoor pursuits were once very important to great numbers of individuals and to the development of Wisconsin society and culture. Perhaps these stories will inspire current and future generations to take up trout fishing or duck hunting or to realize that a vacation to the northwoods can be as satisfying as a vacation to anywhere else in the world.

I think the old-timers would like that.

The making of a good fish story, Ross' Teal Lake Lodge WHi Image ID 37954

Chapter 1
Fish Stories

Fishing is certainly one of the oldest recreational activities in human history. Following close behind is telling stories about fishing. Through the years "fish stories" have often made the pages of Wisconsin newspapers and magazines. A Rhinelander-area newspaper, *The New North*, ran this story in 1912:

The best fish story of the season comes from Three Lakes. The tale was sworn to before a justice of the peace by John Smith, a witness. John Barry, a Chicago banker, was the angler.

Barry was fishing with a small hook for bait. A minnow became fastened on the hook. A one pound black bass spied the minnow and grabbed him whereupon a large "musky" observed Mr. Bass and swallowed hook, minnow, and bass. By careful maneuvering and expert skill Barry landed the finny trio—three fish on one hook. [1]

Another "multiple-fish" story from Three Lakes, this one in 1965, was reported by the *Rhinelander Daily News*:

Dale Bruss, new English teacher and assistant basketball coach at the high school here, hooked a 12- or 13-inch northern and landed an 18 pound, five ounce musky instead, Friday.

Bruss was fishing in Range Line Lake and hooked the northern, with a small daredevil, but "everything became a blur" when a musky, evidently chasing the northern, jumped into the boat.

"I dropped my pole and picked up an oar to kill the musky," said Bruss. He managed to daze the fish long enough to get to shore where he and a neighbor used a gaff hook and gaffed the fish. [2]

Muskies were often the subjects of northwoods newspaper reports. In 1914 a northern Wisconsin newspaper carried the story with the exciting headline: "Big Fish Swamps Boat: Two Fishermen Nearly Drown While Trying to Land Musky." The article went on to describe the perilous event:

While attempting to land a giant muskallonge [sic] Saturday afternoon Leon Gorman and Fred Pecor had a narrow escape from drowning in the Wisconsin River near Rainbow Rapids.

Mesrrs. Gorman and Pecor were trolling in a row boat when the former gentleman hooked the big fish. In the battle which followed the boat tipped over, throwing the occupants into the stream. Both would probably have lost their lives had not a nearby fisherman in another boat hurried to their rescue.[3]

The musky was lost, but Gorman related that "it was the largest muskallonge [sic] he had ever seen . . . it looked to him as huge as a shark."

A big brown trout was the culprit in a near drowning according to a 1937 story in *The Wisconsin Sportsman*:

A tackle-busting old timer, famous in his home territory—North Branch creek, north of Hixton—gave an angler from Melrose a mighty battle on opening day. This big German brown, nine pounds of dynamite, took a smash at an appetizing something or other, only to find it was attached to a rod. Ire aroused, he proceeded to rip around with fervor. The un-named angler, evidently knowing of this grandaddy trout's past tackle-busting history, doubted his own ability to land the fish according to the usual procedure. So he handed his rod to a companion, plunged into the icy water. Grabbing the struggling trout in his arms with much difficulty, he headed for shore. Extremely irked, Mr. Trout summoned up his strength, gave one more big wriggle, tossing the fisherman backwards into deep water, to nearly drown before he was pulled out by bystanders.[4]

A fish of a different sort, not usually known for an aggressive nature, was responsible for chasing two young fishermen from their boat, according to another *Wisconsin Sportsman* report in 1937:

It happened near Oakwood Beach on Lake Winnebago, this genesis of a whopper of a fish story. Harry Mitchell and Robert Kramer, both 14, were rowing along in their boat when a huge fish leaped out of the water and landed in their craft. Startled and confused, both boys leaped from the boat to the comparative safety of the fish's own backyard—the lake. Recovering from their fright, the boys mustered up courage to ease back to the boat to investigate. They found a large carp still floundering around in the bottom of the boat, which they pushed to shore, where they dumped the 12½ pound specimen which soon they were exhibiting with pride. The incident sets some sort of record it is believed.[5]

A "battling wall-eyed pike" chased a woman not only from her boat but completely off Lake Mendota, according to another report from 1937: "Charging that a battling wall-eyed pike chased her off Lake Mendota after she hit him with an oar, Mrs. Austin Forkner reported that she finally got to the beach, landed the 30-inch specimen with a net."[6]

In the days before it was common to see women in the outdoors, stories of angling feats by females often made headlines.

In 1908 the *Wausau Daily Record-Herald* ran a story with the attention-getting headline: "Killed Big Musky with a Club: And the Slayer Was a Woman, Too, Doing It All Alone."

The fact that a woman was fishing alone and actually caught a large musky without male assistance was big news back then.

"To say a woman killed a thirty-two pound muscalonge [sic] with a club sounds fishy as a story, but Mrs. M. C. Thorn has the fish at her home at Riverview park on exhibition to prove her story, so it must be accepted, especially since it is told by a fair angler," the newspaper reported.[7]

More than thirty years later, women anglers were still making headlines in Wausau.

In 1940 the *Daily Record-Herald* reported: "Fisherwoman Lands Two Fish at a Time."

Mrs. William Jahsman . . . has proved herself a two-fisted angler.

Last Thursday, she was after the big ones in Lake Alice, near Heafford Junction, using two cane poles.

11

A 20-pound northern pike, which was 40 inches long, hit the bait on one pole, and as Mrs. Jahsman was preparing to haul it in, another northern hit the bait of pole No. 2.

With a bit of maneuvering, Mrs. Jahsman hauled in both of them. The second fish was 25 inches long and weighed 3½ pounds.

For skeptical anglers of the stronger sex, the fish are on display at the Northland Sporting Goods store.[8]

In more recent times there was an ongoing rumor about a monster musky haunting the waters of Lake Minocqua, according to the local papers during the summer of 1977.

"The rumor around Minocqua area this week is of a fish that took five hours to fight, but still got away," reported Ed Wodalski of *Rhinelander Daily News*. A local sporting goods dealer told Wodalski, "There have been other sightings of a large musky in the area that could go over 100 pounds, but more reasonable estimates might be 60 pounds, not 100 pounds. That sounds pretty fishy."[9]

Several weeks later, some thought they had the explanation.

"The monster muskie controversy in Minocqua Lake has had some new light shed on it this past week," Wodalski reported. "It appears that the fish may not have been a muskie at all but rather a lake sturgeon."[10]

Fish stories, whether true, half true, or bonafide "whoppers," have kept us intrigued and entertained for decades. The Wisconsin fishing experience just wouldn't be the same without these tales of courage, drama, and amazement that come from our lakes and rivers. Heard a good one lately?

The *Viking* Courtesy of Laurel Edwards

T o say that Donald "Ducky" Reed has strong family ties to the Bay Shore of Oconto, the small Wisconsin city found near the bottom of the stair-step-shaped county of the same name where it meets the waters of Green Bay, would be an understatement. He can, in fact, look back to his great-great-grandparents—early settlers who arrived in Oconto in the spring of 1856 by way of steamship from Chicago.[1]

His great-grandfather, Louis Reed, was born in Hamburg, Germany, in 1841. In 1846, his family came to America, making the forty-two-day voyage from Hamburg to New York City in a sailing vessel.[2] They settled in Chicago, where young Louis was educated in the public schools for ten years. Louis was just a teen-ager when his parents packed up their belongings and headed up the western shore of Lake Michigan toward what they hoped would be great opportunity at the small community of Oconto. Wisconsin had become a state only eight years before.

The Reed family was heading to a location already steeped in history. An ancient Indian burial ground considered to be the oldest cemetery in Wisconsin dating to 6,000–5,000 BC, today the location of Copper Culture State Park, is located along the Oconto River on the west side of present-day Oconto.[3] Nicolas Perrot, the first French trader in the region, was said to have mediated a dispute between the Potawatomi and the Menominee near the present site of Oconto in the 1660s. During the winter of 1669–1670, French Jesuit missionary Father Claude-Jean Allouez said mass at a mixed village of Sauk, Potawatomi, Fox, and Winnebago (Ho-Chunk) on the Oconto River at the site of present-day Oconto.[4] One of the first white settlers, Robert Jones, built two sawmills on the Oconto River in 1851.[5] At this time only six families called Oconto their home. A June 10, 1909, retrospective in the *Oconto County Reporter* described the young village back in the early 1850s: "Oconto at this time, was only a woods with

Indian trails running through, the main trail extending from the water mill to the mouth of the river along what is now Main Street. The Indians had their camps along this trail."[6]

When the Reeds arrived at Oconto the settlement was in the midst of transforming from a pioneer outpost to a growing lumber town. The bay allowed access to the old-growth pine lands of northeastern Wisconsin and the rivers—the Peshtigo, Menominee, and Oconto—a way to get the logs to sawmills. The mills transformed what seemed like a limitless supply of raw logs into lumber to feed the insatiable demands of Chicago, which was growing at an astronomical rate. Rafts loaded with finished lumber would be towed to the mouth of the river and then loaded onto sailing vessels for transport south.[7]

Not long after his arrival, Louis Reed found work in a lathe mill, and he also worked as a carpenter, helping to build the first Oconto County courthouse.[8] With early Oconto industry centering on the logging and lumber business, Reed readily found employment as a log driver and lumberjack. He drove for thirteen seasons, having charge of the drive for five.[9]

While Oconto sawmills were turning out pine lumber, the commercial fishing industry was growing, quickly becoming the town's second leading industry.

As with many men in the area, Reed worked in the woods during the winter and engaged in commercial fishing on the bay in the summer.

Turning more and more to the bay for livelihood, he began living on the South Bay Shore in the 1860s. The home Reed built on a tract of land on the shore of Green Bay south of Oconto would become a focal point for generations of Reeds to come, referred to simply as the "Big Bay House" or the "Old House" by the family.

Reed married Jane Gale, the daughter of Abram and Harriet Gale, who had moved their family to Oconto from Oshkosh in 1854. Abram had acquired a Swampland Grant from the government in 1856 that consisted of a mile and a half of Green Bay shoreline south of the Oconto River.[10] Abram Gale later deeded this property to Louis and Jane, and it is probably where Louis Reed built the Big Bay House, but this is unclear.

Ducky Reed described the early Reed commercial fishing operations: "The early fishing was with sailboats and pound nets [pronounced *pond* nets—a stationary net held in place by stakes]. In the winter they set pound nets through the ice using horses. Whitefish and herring were the main catch back then. They would salt the fish in barrels at the fish houses to be shipped by the railroads, going to Chicago and other places. Men worked for a dollar a day and were fed at the house."[11]

As Louis Reed's family grew, the house on the bay grew, too.

"Louis built additions to the house as the family grew," said Ducky. "They had seven children. The oldest was my grandmother, Eva Reed Holmes. She died two days after giving birth to my father, Everett."

Ducky explained how he kept the Reed family name: "My father was raised by my grandmother's sister, and he took to the name Reed, eventually having his last name of Holmes legally changed to Reed."

Everett Reed carried on the family's commercial fishing tradition. Louis and Jane transferred the bay shore property to Everett in 1921. In 1927 he married Florence May Johnson, and a third generation of Reeds began life in the big house with the birth of Ducky (whose nickname came from the popular Disney cartoon character, Donald Duck, which debuted in 1934) in 1930.

Growing up in a commercial fishing family with Green Bay in the backyard made for an interesting childhood. "My father built two fishing boats behind the house," said Ducky. "The first was the *Viking*, built [in 1929] before I was born."

The *Viking*, at thirty-nine feet, was typical of the wooden gill net fish "tugs" that had been developed for the Great Lakes. When the *Viking* was completed, it was launched directly into the bay from its perch in the maple grove on the beach in the backyard of the Big Bay House.

As commercial fishing boats transformed from the two-masted Mackinaw sailboats used in the early days to steam-powered and then diesel-powered engines, the boats took on the familiar look of Great Lakes fish tugs with enclosed decks for protection from the weather and a prominent pilot house. The gill net was the mainstay of the industry, more cost effective than pound nets and able to catch fish in deeper water.

Commercial fishing on Green Bay in the 1930s was primarily for herring, lake trout, yellow perch, and suckers—the whitefish sought in earlier days having been overfished. While the herring catch had also declined from its 1905 peak, fishing the fall herring run could still be a profitable venture. In the fall of 1930, the *Viking* had a record herring catch of twelve thousand pounds in one day, according to Ducky. When herring catches also began to plummet in the late 1930s beyond the point of profitability for the small operator, due in part from increasing pollution from paper mills, the *Viking* was relegated to dry dock and eventually sold.

A more optimistic commercial fishing outlook, particularly for yellow perch, in the early 1940s prompted Everett Reed to begin construction on a second fishing tug, the *Buccaneer*. While most of the new fishing tugs were being built of steel by the 1940s, the *Buccaneer* would be a traditional wooden boat because it was not being built in a commercial shipyard with access to metalworking and welding equipment.

Ducky remembers how his father began work on the boat after January in the winter of 1943: "The *Buccaneer* was built behind the house, like the *Viking*. Dad started cutting white oak that winter up north because around here, we have mostly red oak. He cut two-and-one-quarter-inch square strips while the wood was green, which were then soaked in a tank of hot water and bent to make the ribs. After bending them they would put them on a flat wood surface, using blocking to hold them till they were dry enough. He made them in pairs, so each pair was exactly alike for each side of the boat. He had the size of each pair of ribs drawn out on paper. The cabin was constructed by local homebuilders Hansen & Strutz. She had a sharp bow with a covering of galvanized steel up to the waterline which was needed to break ice."

As with many of the Green Bay fishing tugs it had a twin-cylinder Kahlenberg engine in it. "The engine had built-in blowtorches to heat up the cylinders, and then compressed air would start it," Ducky remembered.

The forty-four-foot *Buccaneer* hit the water in the backyard of the Big Bay House as perch fishing in the bay peaked. "In spring of 1943, the first year out, a crew of five men picked twenty-five hundred to three thousand pounds of perch a day while father had to stay in the wheelhouse to keep the boat from going over the net," said Ducky. "At eight to ten cents a pound, my dad was able to pay off the $2,100 loan for the boat that same year in December."

The perch boom didn't last long, and catches began to decline by 1945, just two years after the peak. "The *Buccaneer* was sold to fisherman Norbert Frasch from Two Rivers. It broke up on the rocks inside the breakwater there when the engine stopped during a storm," said Ducky.

With the overall decline of the Green Bay fishery, compounded by the arrival of the sea lamprey, Everett Reed focused his business efforts on a successful mink ranch from 1946 till 1968. "When the mink were no longer profitable, my dad bought a Lake Erie steel gill net boat in 1967. He converted it into a trawler and named it the *Bounty*," said Ducky.

"He trawled for alewife on Green Bay, which were sold to Art Swaer's fish meal plant, Schilling Fish, on the Pensaukee River where the *Bounty* was harbored. My daughter, Laurel, and I also fished with the *Bounty*," said Ducky. "When the alewife were no longer plentiful on Green Bay, he took the trawler to Sheboygan and installed a lifter for gill nets and fished for chubs that winter from Sheboygan. I stayed back home and finished pelting out the remaining mink to ship to the New York auction."

In 1979, Everett sold the *Bounty* to Schilling Fish in Pensaukee. Owner Art Swaer changed the boat's name to *Art Swaer IV* and continued trawling for alewife there until he gave the boat to longtime employee John Kulpa, who converted it back to a gill net boat. Kulpa still fishes perch with it from the Pensaukee River.[12]

Everett passed away at the age of eighty-six in 1990 and his wife, Florence, in 1994, leaving the Big Bay House to their children, Ducky and Janice.

Today, Ducky Reed's only daughter, Laurel Edwards, and her family occupy the Big Bay House—and Laurel's daughter, Megan, represents the fifth generation of Reed descendents to have lived there. Ducky lives in a small house next door to the old house. The large picture window in the living room of Ducky's home frames a scene of beach and Green Bay open water that one could imagine has changed little since 1856 when the steamship carrying sixteen-year-old Louis Reed passed the spot on its way to his new home.

Todd Sheldon with a stringer of Mepps-caught fish Courtesy of Mike Sheldon

Chapter 3
The Mepps Story

T he fact that the world headquarters of one of the most successful fishing lure companies of all time can be found right downtown in the small Wisconsin community of Antigo has always intrigued me. I had heard bits and pieces of the fascinating decades-old story of Sheldons', Inc., owners of the Mepps brand of French spinner, but I wanted to know more. Curious, I ventured to the rather inconspicuous Mepps building on Antigo's north side. The sign on Highway 45 that states "Squirrel Tails Wanted" is the only tip-off to the company's location.

I found company president J. M. "Mike" Sheldon in his office. The room had changed little since his late father and company founder A. L. "Todd" Sheldon occupied it. The trophy fish adorning the walls and the full-body mounts of brown and polar bears were testament to Todd Sheldon's love of fishing and hunting. The senior Sheldon, who passed away in 1995 at age eighty-one, was able to combine his love of the outdoors with his considerable business talents to create a fishing lure empire.

When Todd Sheldon graduated from Antigo High School in 1931, he had no idea that his life would one day be devoted to a fishing lure. At that moment, adventure was on his mind as he threw in a few dollars with four friends to buy an ancient Model T, the vehicle that would take the boys across a 1930s American west.

Upon his return, Sheldon found his hometown immersed in the greatest economic collapse the country had ever seen. Small towns in northern Wisconsin held little promise for the young men of the Great Depression. In 1935, as did thousands of other young men, he was fortunate to find employment with the Civilian Conservation Corps (CCC). Sheldon worked at Camp Elcho, about twenty miles north of Antigo. The CCC boys at the camp spent long days working on white pine blister rust control, and in return they received a little hard cash. [1]

As the country pulled itself out of the Great Depression and into World War II, Sheldon found himself working for the war effort at a factory in Milwaukee. After the war he returned to Antigo to pursue a dream he had of owning a sporting goods store. In 1948 he opened Sheldon's Sport Shop on Superior Street in downtown Antigo. At about this same time Sheldon was introduced to the little spinner that was destined to change his life.

"After the war most soldiers brought home a few French spinners," explained Mike Sheldon. "A man named Frank Velak had given some to Dad after he returned from Europe." Apparently the elder Sheldon put them in his tackle box and proceeded to forget about them for two years. The story might have ended there if fate had not intervened in the form of a bad day's fishing. The "rest of the story" has been retold countless times and is now the cornerstone of Mepps lore.

According to the story, Todd was having a bad day fishing on the Wolf River in 1951, and after rummaging in his tackle box to find something that might work, he found one of the Mepps given to him by Velak, and he tied it on. To his amazement he began pulling in fat trout. He was immediately sold on the lure.

The Mepps "aglia" spinner was the invention of Frenchman Andre Muelnart, who registered his design in 1938. Mepps was the French acronym for the name of Muelnart's lure-making factory, translated as the "Manufacturer of Precision Equipment for Sport Fishing." Another Frenchman, Ferdinand Helias, was a silent partner.

Sheldon began selling the lures at his sport shop. Velak supplied the spinners through an unusual arrangement, another important piece of Mepps lore. Velak received his lures from a French woman he had met during the war in exchange for supplying her with American nylons. The arrangement worked for several years, until the demand for Mepps spinners began to outpace the woman's need for nylons.

In the early 1960s the Mepps owners in France replaced Velak with George Boehm, who formed a supplier-distributor partnership with Sheldon. By this time the potential for Mepps sales in the United States was becoming clear—sport fishing was becoming big business, and anglers were spending more and more money on fishing tackle. In a self-serving move to gain complete control over U.S. Mepps sales, Boehm pulled a dirty trick and convinced the Mepps owners to oust Sheldon from the company. However, Sheldon had previously acquired exclusive rights to sell the French spinner in the United States. The tables turned on Boehm as he discovered he had no legal outlet for Mepps sales in the United States. Todd Sheldon's business genius triumphed, and he later bought out Boehm.

Several years later, the aging owners of Mepps, Muelnart and Helias, decided to sell their interests in the company to Sheldon, and in 1973 Sheldons', Inc., became the sole owner of Mepps.

"Mepps is still a French operation," said Mike Sheldon. "Most of the manufacturing still occurs in France. Most of the assembly of the spinner components, packaging, and shipping take place in Antigo."

Though the lure is French, Todd Sheldon was responsible for an American "stamp" on Muelnart's spinner: the addition of squirrel or buck tail. Sheldon was fishing on the Wolf when he ran into a young boy who had caught some very nice trout on a lure adorned with squirrel tail hair. Sheldon immediately began to experiment with adding dressing of animal hair to Mepps spinners. The results were incredibly successful, and the rest, as they say, is history.

"We still use natural squirrel or buck tail today," said Mike Sheldon. "We have tried other types of animal hair, such as fox, coyote, and skunk, as well as synthetic material, but nothing works as well." Sheldon added, "But squirrel tails are getting harder to come by, because not as many people are out hunting squirrels."

Sheldons' has raised the price they pay for squirrel tails, from ten cents in 1970 to around twenty cents today. "We could pay more, but we don't want people to hunt squirrels just to sell the tail," said Sheldon.

Through the years Todd Sheldon continued to test new ideas and designs as he fished all over the world, particularly in northern Canada and Alaska. He fished familiar waters close to home as well. "We had a cottage on Post Lake," said Mike Sheldon, "and Dad fished there frequently. He also liked to fish the Menominee Indian Reservation."

In his later years, Todd Sheldon still went into the office every day he was able, and he remained involved in company operations. When a friend invited him to play a little golf, Sheldon replied, "Golf is for old men!"

Since Todd Sheldon's death the company has maintained the strong focus he established, but some changes have taken place.

"We decided to stop advertising and instead utilize company representatives to promote the product," said Mike Sheldon. "We came to realize that working with real fishermen is the best way to make Mepps known."

Already a household name within any home of someone who fishes, the Mepps spinner needs little promotion. Since the first few spinners sold by Todd Sheldon at the sports store in the 1950s, Sheldons', Inc., has sold more than 350 million fishing lures. There are few tackle boxes in America that don't contain at least one Mepps spinner. In 1984 Todd Sheldon was inducted into the Freshwater Fishing Hall of Fame at Hayward as a "Legendary Angler" for his business genius and commitment to the sport of fishing.

A late 1800s trout fishing expedition on the Brule River WHi Image ID 2206

Chapter 4
Trouting on the Brule:
An 1875 Fishing Expedition to
Northern Wisconsin and Michigan

T
o find a real wilderness hunting or fishing experience these days many
Midwestern sports enthusiasts travel to the Rocky Mountains or to Alaska
or Canada. In the 1870s, however, those with a thirst for big adventure
in the wild needed only to go as far as northern Wisconsin or the Upper
Peninsula of Michigan.

Three lawyers and a businessman from Chicago found more than their share
of rugged outdoor adventure when they mounted an expedition to the wild
border lands of northeast Wisconsin and Michigan's Upper Peninsula in 1875.
The attorneys, John Lyle King, James L. High, and Josiah H. Bissell, along with
businessman Lorenzo Pratt, took to the northwoods "for an excursion, and on a
vacation furlough" in August of that year.

Their destination was the Brule River, which for most of its forty-five-mile
length serves as the Wisconsin-Michigan border in Forest and Florence counties,
Wisconsin, and Iron County, Michigan.

Thankfully for all of us today who are fascinated with Wisconsin and
Michigan sporting history, the members of the party had the forethought to
keep detailed journals of their 1875 expedition and a second expedition in 1877,
which in turn served as the basis for a book written by King: *Trouting on the Brule
River: Or Summer-Wayfaring in the Northern Wilderness*, published in 1880.[1]

Early in the book King described the river of their desire: "This river of trout,
the Brule or Boise Brule, is a small, clear, cold, rocky stream of sixty miles, issuing
from Lake Brule, running south by east. Not far from its mouth it is joined by the
Paint river, and their commingled waters flowing for another four or five miles,
and then receiving another affluent, the Michigamic [Michigamme] river, as
blended tributaries become thence the Menominee river."

By providing an extremely detailed account of expeditions to the Brule or what he calls the "Boise [sic] Brule" (he probably has in mind here the Bois Brule in Douglas County), King inadvertently, or perhaps purposefully, preserved forever a vision of a northeastern Wisconsin that existed for only a short time—the period after the start of big pine logging but before its peak and plummeting decline. King and his group were able to witness the scarred cutover as well as the raw wilderness of the virgin forest.

Ironically it was the inroads the logging and mining industries were making in the north during this period that allowed the party access, through rail and haul roads, to the edge of a huge chunk of wild country where conventional travel gave way to the necessity of Indian guides and birch bark canoes but within a generation would transform the north into something much less wild and exciting.

King—with a lawyer's skill for written detail, a keen sense of humor, and a deep appreciation for what he was experiencing—was able to put on paper much more than just a routine account of the trip.

In the preface to *Trouting*, King alluded to the idea that although their goal may have been a fantastic trout fishing experience, there was more to it than that: "When the haunts of game in the woods and the lairs of fish in the streams incite the passion for sport to couple itself with the quest and yearning for rest and vitalization, the wayfarer's pathway in the wilderness becomes a pilgrimage through abounding scenes of diversion and into a realm of fascination."

Planning and making arrangements for the expedition did not seem to be a terribly complicated affair. The trip to the Brule consisted of three main components—the train ride north, a horse-drawn wagon to haul gear overland, and birch bark canoes for the river.

King wrote: "The outfit and supplies were provided in Chicago, and sent by the Chicago & Northwestern railway to Section Eighteen, a station of that road eighteen miles beyond Marinette, Wisconsin. The other accessories—a team for the land route and the guides—were engaged in advance at Marinette, and met the party at Section Eighteen. The canoes were to be procured at Badwater, on the Menominee, where the water travel began."

King gave his readers the impression that anyone with a desire to enjoy the sporting opportunities that the Wisconsin and Michigan northwoods had to offer could do so if they had sufficient time, funds, and the health and stamina for roughing it. King himself was fifty-two years of age during the first Brule River expedition—a relatively advanced age for the 1870s.

Trouting on the Brule: An 1875 Fishing Expedition
to Northern Wisconsin and Michigan

After what was about a sixteen-hour trip from Chicago on the Chicago & Northwestern rails, the party found themselves and their gear at Section Eighteen on August 10, 1875.

King wrote: "The eighteenness of the section was the most there was of it—that is, its being that distance in miles from Menominee. The rest—the odds and ends of it—was a small, rude, uncovered log platform, with a log cabin and a little wheezing steam sawmill in the background of a bit of a clearing in the woods."

At this primitive whistle-stop they met George Evanson, the teamster they had hired to haul themselves and their outfit to the Menominee River at Badwater. Evanson was "a tough Norwegian, with a span of rugged, stout horses."

Also waiting for the party at Section Eighteen were the two Menominee Indian guides, George Kaquotash and Mitchell Thebault.

"They were coated, trowsered and booted in backwoods attire," observed King. "They were stalwart, and seemingly in superb order for our purposes."

Leaving behind the comfort of railcar, the four sportsmen, their guides, and the teamster started off toward the Brule on a haul road that was "rough and up and down." A steady rain soaked everyone, and the summer foliage was dripping.

"We had arranged our time-table to make Peemony farm for the night," wrote King. "The showers, however, rather abated the ardor of advance."

The group decided to spend the night at "The Relay House," eight miles distant from the railroad, where a roaring stove quickly began to dry wet clothes.

The Relay House was only a half mile from the Menominee River, and after supper the party hiked there "for a glimpse of river scenery."

It was along the river where they discovered a large, abandoned cabin with a "ghostly inmate" inside. A Catholic priest and companion had holed up in the cabin to escape the rain. The pair was traveling upriver for deer hunting. "It was evident that the consecrated sportsman loved to handle a weapon that was not spiritual, as well as to twiddle a rosary," King wrote.

The rain continued through the night and into the next day, but the sportsmen accepted the bad weather with good spirits.

"We tried to tickle ourselves with mirth, and to weather it, or volatilize the exceeding moisture and ourselves with dry jokes. We jested at the rain while it was pelting us," wrote King.

As the rain continued the road "worsened greatly."

King wrote: "The roughness of the road added greatly to the mishaps of the rain. There was nowhere a level more than a few rods. By way of variety of misery, some or all of us got out and walked, and soon, as we trod along, our boots or shoes were soaked like sponges, and squshed [sic] the water up our shins and knees."

After a day of traveling "over corduroy, and pitching into holes and ruts" the group arrived at their destination for the day, a logging camp known as Stephenson's.

"It was a large, double, low, pine log and logmen's cabin of the most primitive frontier order of architecture," wrote King. "Interiorly, it was fitted up roughly but comfortably, for the needs of the hardy choppers, whose axes make annual havoc in the neighboring forests of pine."

Because it was summer, there were only two or three people at the camp, one of them the camp cook.

"Of all the Stephensonian denizens, the cook was the most important personage to us," wrote King. "He was a shiny faced, stumpy young French Canadian, with a patois of Quebec and Boston."

The sportsmen from Chicago were then treated to a regular logging camp supper of pork, biscuits, potatoes, and coffee. "The spread gratifyingly surprised and satisfied us," wrote King.

While the rain continued outside, the party contented themselves with tending to their gear, smoking pipes, and reading novels in the warmth of the cabin.

"The situation, for one of weather-bound confinement, was not, by any means, intolerable."

The next day brought improved weather, and the party "bid adieu" to Stephenson's camp and made their way through miles of dense forest eventually passing by the clearing of another camp, Sturgeon Farm (also known as New York Farm).

Some miles later the expedition encountered an abandoned logging camp, and King succinctly described the view of the cutover: "We plodded on till we reached a hill range overlooking the river. There was an open space from which the timber had been cleanly stripped, and a deserted cabin then in decay, was the sole vestige of a former busy logging camp. The ground was worthless for culture, but had a great apparent capacity for brambles and weeds. And when its original wealth of pines had been exhausted, the place was abandoned and relapsed into a dismal waste."

Trouting on the Brule: An 1875 Fishing Expedition to Northern Wisconsin and Michigan

The third night since setting out from Section Eighteen was spent at a frontier trading station known as "Dickey's."

"It [Dickey's] serves as a domicile, as a store in a rudimentary form, and as a hostelry or inn, in a legal sense, as a place where the traveler is furnished with everything he wants, provided the traveler has occasion for very little," observed King.

One item of interest to the party that Dickey's did have on hand was a birch bark canoe, although they had arranged for canoes to be available at Badwater.

"It occurring to us that as a bird in the hand is worth more than the possible or uncertain bird or dozen birds in the bush, a canoe we could secure was more valuable and to our purpose than supposed or conjectural canoes up the river, we advised ourselves to invest in the present vessel," explained King.

They purchased the canoe for twenty dollars and christened it *The Dickey*.

The ten miles of road from Dickey's to Badwater were the most primitive of the trip, degenerating into a rough trail, and progress was slow due to swamps and bogs and numerous fallen trees blocking the path that had to be chopped out of the way.

"Towards the close of the day and the end of the route, difficulties provokingly multiplied. The timber across the trail appeared to be larger and plentier, and the chopping more laborious."

Darkness overtook them while they were still battling the trail, and an impromptu campsite had to be found by candlelight. The generally high spirits of the sportsmen were severely tested that night by swarms of mosquitoes.

"We could well have resigned ourselves to the situation, were it not that the same camp-fire which brightened us was a signal for the mosquitoes to swarm upon us for an eager reception."

However, a well-received camp supper prepared by one of the guides was pronounced a "happy success."

The next morning the party reached the Indian settlement of Badwater and was unloaded near the banks of the Menominee River. Evanson turned his team around and headed home with an empty wagon.

King described what he observed: "Small meadows on either side [of the river], with five or six rude Indian cabins scattered over them, all but one on the Michigan shore, were the vista before us, called Badwater."

The Badwater Indian village was located on a bend in the Menominee River in the Spread Eagle chain of lakes. The small Wisconsin town of Spread Eagle lies in the vicinity of where Badwater once existed.

At Badwater the party engaged the services of Tom King, a well-known Ojibwa, as a third guide. They also bought a birch bark canoe from King for fifteen dollars, christened the *Tom King*.

The four Chicago sportsmen and their three Indian guides traveled by canoe up the Menominee to the mouth of the Michigamme River. At this point excitement coursed through the party as they were nearly to the Brule after four days and three nights of rugged travel.

"By overland, the distance is three miles to Brule Falls, while by river it is seven miles," King wrote. The group decided to send their gear via water on the *Dickey*, their largest canoe, with guides Thebault and Kaquotash. They would accompany Tom King as he portaged the smaller canoe overland. "We were eager to reach the river of trout sooner than we could by the water ascent," wrote King.

"Bissell was ambitious to catch the first glimpse of the stream which was the longed-for scene of our sport, and with this aspiration as an accelerating impulse, kept the extreme front of the line of march. When at length, he vociferously shouted 'Brule! Brule!' we huzzaed him back an uproarious answer, 'The Brule! The Brule!'"

After many days of hard travel the expedition members finally arrived at their destination, the Brule River, and were eager to begin catching trout.

"The fishermen were ready for a trial of the rod at the very first. Eagerness became enthusiasm, and the party, excepting myself, at once sought places in which to throw their flies," wrote King.

King, who was actually an avid bass fisherman and had never gone trout fishing prior to the Brule expedition, surveyed the area and came across a tent camp with three men playing cards. The two groups quickly acquainted themselves with each other. King's party learned that the men had been camped on the Brule for a week, having ventured only about six or seven miles upstream with limited success.

King wrote: "Our care was, then, to pack up and pack off. Our mission of sport would be not really begun until we were on the bosom of the Brule." The group decided to make camp with their new friends that night and head upstream the next day.

Trouting on the Brule: An 1875 Fishing Expedition
to Northern Wisconsin and Michigan

Heading upstream after breakfast in the morning, the party fished as they traveled, with few results. "But, after lunch, and an hour further on, the luring fly began to strike the responsive fish," wrote King.

King, sporting a stiff eighteen-ounce bass fishing rod, tried his hand at trouting for the first time. "I stepped out on the rock, and cast a fresh fly. In a twinkling it was snatched at, and to my surprise, I had really struck a trout of dimensions, as was plain from the lively struggle it made," wrote King. "But I brought him in. It was about a fourteen-ouncer. It was the first trout I ever caught. The achievement brought down the house, and the whole party huzzaed with a will."

The second night on the Brule the group camped "on a high, steep grassy bank. At a bend, and with a space, under immense trees, already cleared for prior camps."

"We had made a fair start in trouting," wrote King with his usual flair. "The record of the day, not so much for its count—fifty-five—but as a promise of better yet to come, a catching that was but a cheering prologue to the more lavish performance that was to follow, was eminently satisfactory."

Continual rain and oppressive mosquitoes plagued the group at their nightly camps. "The mosquitoes burdened the air with their songs, but the oil and tar with which we copiously anointed ourselves served to repel them to respectful distance, until, at least, the malodorous unguent lost its effect, and then the slicking was repeated," King explained.

However, despite hardships of travel, location, and weather, the group remained in awe of the wilderness they found themselves in, such a difference from the hustle of city life. King wrote: "If we had needed more than the oppressive stillness, the deep shadows and heavy foliage which overspread us, to remind us that we were in the wilds of nature, the howl of a wolf which we heard in the distance would have been assurance enough."

On Monday, the group's fourth day on the Brule, they broke camp and headed upstream, this time with clear skies and the promise of good weather, the first of the trip. Their destination was a place called "Windfall," fifteen miles upstream from the Brule's mouth and so named because "a tornado had leveled the forest at some not remote period."

Again, the men fished as they traveled upstream, with results improving with each mile gained. "The baskets were plentifully replenished, and with choicer spoils, on the average, than those of previous sport," wrote King.

While the fishing improved, the promise of good weather did not hold as clouds began to form and rain once again soaked the expedition.

The return of wet conditions was offset by great fishing success. "Spite of the day's adverse conditions, though, we could compute sensations of pleasure to an aggregate of one hundred and forty-five, for the party, those being the figures of joint capture," wrote King happily.

King, the bass fisherman, found that pieces of a passenger pigeon killed earlier by Pratt worked wonders on Brule River trout but raised the ire of High, one of the true trout fishermen in the group.

"This sort of fishing was an abomination, and utterly immitigable, to High," explained King. "It was bait-fishing, and baiting for trout, whether the bait were worm, flesh, fowl, fish or natural insect, or whatever else, was simply a gross and vulgar folly." With meals of trout for breakfast, lunch, and dinner seemingly assured, while camped at Windfall the party learned a lesson about food security in the north. King wrote: "While we slept, the enemy came and despoiled us of the breakfast mess. The pick of the day's trout had been dressed, and laid out over night in beautiful array, on the provision box, right close to the nostrils of George, where he must have been frightfully snoring, as was his wont, under the canoe. The minks stole a march on the sleeping sentinel at his post, and made a foray on the fish, and portaged the entire lot to their holes."

While the group's stay at Windfall camp provided exceptional trout fishing, along with improved weather, food staples such as pork, potatoes, and lard began to run low. "To retrace our course was, therefore, a necessity," wrote King, "but a much regretted one."

Now on the long journey back to Chicago, the men, as was tradition at the time, carved their names and information about their fishing success into the bark of trees at each of their previous campsites. Forsaking their original wagon route and the misery of traveling over the rough roads, they finally reached Menominee, Michigan, by canoe.

"We reached Menominee at noon," wrote King. "The vacation ramble ended there; canoeing on the streams and tenting in the forests, our open air life, were to be, thence, only memories; but with us, memories always golden and abiding."

Fishermen with Caille outboard Courtesy of Jack Craib

Chapter 5

Lost Outboard Recovered
after Seventy Years

I n the summer of 1932, resort owner and northwoods fishing guide Harry
Jones lost his prized Caille (pronounced "cail") outboard motor. This Caille
Liberty model outboard, with the long shaft that Jones liked so much because
it enabled great access to shallow bays and creeks, sank to the bottom of
Pickerel Lake near Eagle River in Vilas County.

Daughters Shirley Sleight and Dorothy Uthe, both now living in the small
town of Mercer in Iron County, were just young children at the time, but they
remember the incident as if it happened yesterday.

"We dove into the lake for three days looking for the motor," Uthe recalled.
"But it was never found."[1]

Jones had allowed one of the "sports" at his Pickerel Lake resort to use the
outboard, something he rarely did, according to his daughters. Somehow the
boat rocked or flipped and the motor, not adequately clamped to the boat's
transom, slipped off and sank into the lake.

The story of the lost Caille outboard would have ended there, back in the
summer of 1932, if there hadn't been a stroke of luck that sent the old outboard
on a remarkable odyssey.

After resting more than half a century on the bottom of Pickerel Lake, the
outboard was snagged by a fisherman in the late 1990s and brought to the surface.
Not recognizing the value of the find, the fisherman brought the outboard to the
local dump. From there, the dump custodian, who liked to take home and tinker
with potentially useful items, retrieved the Caille and brought it home.

In a unique coincidence, Dorothy Uthe, a friend of the dump custodian,
stopped by to visit one day and happened to see the old outboard. Uthe immediately recognized the old Caille as the one she and her sister had so diligently
searched for many years before.

The outboard now has come full circle. It has been returned to the family that originally owned it. In amazingly good condition, it is now located at the Mercer Railroad Depot Museum in downtown Mercer, on display for anglers and other visitors to enjoy.

The Detroit-based Caille Perfection Motor Company, founded in 1910, built inboard marine engines, early factory racing outboards, and outboards for fishing boats.[2] The Liberty model's long, direct-drive shaft for fishing boats became a trademark, and the company's advertising slogan for the Liberty was, "Drives your boat where e'er'twill float." A Liberty sold for about seventy-five to eighty-five dollars.

The production of Caille outboards was discontinued in 1935.[3]

Carl Marty feeding a bear cub Courtesy of Wendy Robinson

Chapter 6
Carl Marty's Northernaire:
A Special Place in Time

I t was one of those quirky, rare moments when the convergence of the right place and the right time coalesce into an indelible memory.

I was a senior in high school at the time, and it was the week between Christmas and New Year's. It also was the late 1970s, and cross-country skiing fever had consumed, if not the nation, at least the Upper Midwest. This was the reason behind my parents and I heading north to Eagle River to meet my sister and her family for a long weekend of both skiing and learning how to ski at one of the area resorts.

After a day of the "learning how" part, my parents were ready to move on to something a little less strenuous, something they already knew how to do, and something they were pretty good at—sightseeing, shopping, and eating out.

On this day they had a destination in mind: someplace called the Northernaire. As I pieced together the story during the drive to Three Lakes, in northeast Oneida County, I learned that this Northernaire was nothing short of the "Waldorf of the Wilderness"—a golden, gleaming resort complete with luxury guest rooms, gourmet chefs, a grand ballroom, entertainment that rivaled Las Vegas, and celebrities rubbing elbows with the tourists in the hallways.

My parents had eaten dinner at the Northernaire many years before and had apparently soaked in enough of the grand ambience and aura of the place to create larger-than-life memories that they still held as we pulled into the parking lot that winter afternoon in 1978.

Our car was about the only one in the parking lot. The theme of emptiness continued as we entered the resort and then the well-windowed dining room. Although it was a still a prize week for northern tourism, the Northernaire was quiet, with none of the hustle and bustle you'd expect of a famous northwoods resort. There were no celebrities to rub elbows with. In fact, aside from resort staff, it seemed as if there was no one else in the entire place.

We were seated for lunch in the big dining room, the only people there except for a lone old man sitting at the opposite end of the room. I had noticed him immediately, his presence in the mostly empty dining room conspicuous.

After we ate lunch and my dad paid the bill, the waitress handed me a small paperback book. "Mr. Marty would like you to have this," she said. The book was *Mr. Conservation: Carl Marty and His Forest Orphans*, written by August Derleth, the prolific Wisconsin writer from Sauk City. It was inscribed: "With Best Wishes! Carl Marty."

Then the waitress offered us an invitation on behalf of Mr. Marty to watch some wildlife films. Strange as it may have seemed to me—unfamiliar with Carl Marty or any of the Northernaire's history aside from what my parents had discussed on the short trip from Eagle River to Three Lakes—I immediately said "yes," hoping my parents would agree.

They did, and we were led to a downstairs room where we found the old man I had seen in the dining room, Carl O. Marty Jr. himself, the founder and proprietor of the Northernaire. At that time Marty was nearly eighty years old.

For more than an hour we watched reels of wildlife movies featuring the Northernaire, Marty, and a cast of woodland animals including two otters known as "Sugar and Spice," a beaver named "Bopper," and a porcupine that went by the name of "Ouch."

I didn't realize until many years later that at the time I was experiencing a unique slice of north Wisconsin history as well as playing witness to the end of a special chapter of the northern Wisconsin resort industry.

After learning more about Carl Marty and his vision of a resort unlike any the north had ever seen, I realized that the Northernaire of my parents' memories truly had been something special. But that special place, the reality of the Northernaire as the Waldorf of the Wilderness, existed in a different time—its time the '40s, '50s, and '60s—and by 1978 that time was fairly well past.

Marty was a Wisconsin resort visionary. Born in Monroe, the Swiss cheese capital of the United States, in Green County at the turn of the century, but growing up in Chicago after his father took a job there when Carl was eight, Marty demonstrated his skill in the business world at an early age.[1] In his early twenties he founded "Carl Marty and Company," which specialized in cheese production. Other successful cheese operations, all based in Monroe, followed.[2] By the late 1930s Marty's operations had the attention of milk and cheese giant Borden, which bought him out in 1939.[3]

With money in the bank, Carl Jr., with help from his younger brother Bob, decided to act upon a dream he had of developing the perfect luxury resort.

"The dreaming we had indulged in before, now had to be transferred into practical, business-like plans," Marty wrote in the August 1947 issue of *Resort Management*. "Over a period of time, we had become more and more convinced that there was a definite need in our state of Wisconsin for an all year 'round resort."[4]

Marty knew precisely the type of customer he was after: the more affluent post-war veterans and their baby boomer children. What he would do would be a departure from tradition. He realized that while people desired "new surroundings" for recreation they "would also desire the same comforts, conveniences and luxuries of their town life."[5]

"The people to whom we would appeal, then, would be that class having the time, income and inclination for this kind of resort," wrote Marty. "And in this group are many families with children—youngsters, and young men and women in college and out of school who possess all the vitality and energy of youth accustomed to rigorous activities and sport."[6]

Marty would place his luxury resort in the heart of the northwoods, "where those who seek the outdoors' life and those who wish rest and relaxation may find all this and more among beautiful surroundings and with well-appointed accommodations and efficient service."[7]

Carl Marty Sr. had purchased land on Deer Lake near Three Lakes in 1915 and had built a vacation cottage on it.[8] This area would become the site for Carl Jr.'s dream.

The construction of the Northernaire began in 1946, with the resort formally opening in 1947. The Show Boat night club, which originated as a clubhouse for an existing golf course purchased by the Marty brothers, had already been built and opened in July of 1940. A unique set of circumstances led to the building of Northernaire lore well before the construction of the resort itself.

Professional baseball player Fred "Cy" Williams, who played for the Chicago Cubs and the Philadelphia Phillies during his nineteen-year career from 1912 through the 1920s, had made Three Lakes his permanent home. A capable outfielder, Williams was best known as a home run hitter (the first major leaguer to hit two hundred home runs in his career).

Williams, however, had other talents besides baseball. Before starting with the Cubs he had graduated from Notre Dame with a degree in architecture.[9] When his baseball career had run its course he returned to Three Lakes to begin a successful career in architecture and building. It was natural for Williams to design and build the Northernaire.

Marty's timing for a new kind of northwoods resort could not have been better. Oneida County and other north Wisconsin resort destinations were poised for exceptional growth in the post-war era. In March of 1946 the *Rhinelander Daily News* reported: "All indications here point to the brightest tourist season in Rhinelander's history. Behind the giant wave of optimism sweeping the county's resort men and the Chamber of Commerce is the flood of mail that is engulfing them from the southern part of the state, Illinois and Indiana asking for reservations."[10]

Herman Bostrom, a Rhinelander-area real estate agent and resort owner, offered the *Daily News* his reasoning for the expected influx of tourists: "What makes the tourist prospects rosy, in Bostrom's opinion, is the bulging wallets of the people coupled with a strong yen for relaxation after four years of war and rationing."[11]

The bulging wallet was a key to the future of the Northernaire. If the resort was to supply unparalleled amenities in the northwoods there would be a cost. "This, plus the resort being an all year 'round place, naturally resulted in a cost much higher than average," wrote Marty. "Rates, therefore, had to be keyed commensurate with cost and conveniences offered."[12]

Whether it was pure business savvy, some unexplained intuition, or a little of both, the Marty brothers had hit the mark when determining the clientele they wanted to attract to the Northernaire.

The Waldorf of the Wilderness quickly attracted celebrities as well as well-heeled tourists. In July of 1947 Gypsy Rose Lee, the famous burlesque stripper, actress, and writer, made her second visit to the Northernaire.

"Miss Gypsy Rose Lee, who is vacationing at Marty's near Three Lakes," reported the *Rhinelander Daily News*, "last night showed personal movies to a group of friends and their guests in the Hotel Northernaire and later was presented to guests in Marty's Show Boat."[13]

Lee was an ardent angler: "Miss Lee's personal movies last night showed her fishing expedition last summer near Three Lakes and illustrated in one easy lesson how muskies were landed."

Perhaps more important in the lore and legend, and the fame, of the Northernaire—more than its celebrities and world-class chefs, more than its luxurious amenities and big-city entertainment—were Carl Marty's adopted woodland animals.

"People come here from all over the United States to spend their vacation time among the forests and waters of this magnificent north country. Many are not aware of Carl Marty's fame as a naturalist and are astonished to find small, wild animal orphans wandering at will around the grounds of this luxurious resort," wrote Edith Lassen Johnson in her book about Marty's wild orphans, *Mother Is a Saint Bernard*.[14]

While walking on the Deer Lake property prior to the construction of the resort, Marty and his cocker spaniel Rusty had a brief close encounter with a wild red fox.[15] The incident inspired Marty to experiment with taming wild animals and letting them interact with his domestic pets. Marty started with red fox pups, taming them enough so that they bonded with Rusty. As they grew, the fox were given the freedom to come and go as they pleased, but they seemed to retain an affinity for the spaniel and returned from the woods on numerous visits.

The experience with the fox seemed to rekindle Marty's youthful love of wild-life, and wild animals became a central focus during his reign at the Northernaire. The fox experiment led to deer fawns and eventually to beaver, porcupines, pine marten, and coyotes—just about any orphaned or injured wild animal that was brought to the Northernaire.

Ginger, a daughter of Rusty, along with a St. Bernard named Bernese became famous as the dogs that not only bonded with the wild orphans but mothered, protected, and formed lasting relationships with them.

In a self-published book, *Northernaire's Ginger and Her Woodland Orphans*, Marty writes about building a small house for Ginger:

It was quite evident that Ginger needed a house of her own in which to receive all her woodland friends who come to call. So we had a house built for Ginger with her name on the door, and it has proved to be a popular place for the animals to congregate.

A sign welcomes all animals and says that if the door is closed, to come in through the hole in the floor.

During the summer months especially, Ginger naps heavily during the day because most of her friends come to call at night, and she is kept busy playing the perfect hostess to all![16]

The Northernaire's menagerie of free-roaming wild animals, as well as the celebrity status of Rusty, Ginger, and Bernese, may have done as much to lure tourists to the resort as the scenery, celebrities, and hotel amenities.

Alvin E. O'Konski, a Republican congressman who represented Wisconsin's old tenth district (which covered much of northwestern Wisconsin) was so taken by Marty's wild animal menagerie following visits to the resort that he presented a speech about Marty before the second session of the Ninetieth Congress, subsequently printed in the *Congressional Record*.

In reference to the federal government's spending millions "to find out why rats, mice, and monkeys act the way they do," O'Konski stated:

"For the past 25 years in northern Wisconsin, at no expense to the government, a great humanitarian and a great savior of wildlife has been carrying on exactly such an experiment with no cost to the taxpayers. He has learned why wild animals act the way they do. He has discovered a way of getting the animals of the forest to accept each other, to live with each other, and to love each other."[17]

With a protectionist outlook on wild animals, Carl Marty was not the best friend of the local hunters and trappers. Some of his friends included Cleveland Amory and Sterling North, noted antihunting and antitrapping figures. But they also included outdoorsmen-writers—such as nationally known Sigurd Olson and local Walt Goldsworthy—as well as Rhinelander-area woodsman and trapper Paul Munninghoff.

Goldsworthy's widow, Doris, told me that Marty was vehemently opposed to trapping and angered local residents with his push to establish no-hunting and no-trapping refuge areas around Three Lakes. "He didn't like the idea that animals such as beaver could be trapped when the kits were in the den," she said.[18]

The Northernaire as a business entity, however, was not by any means against animal use.

The first issue of *Northernaire and Showboat News*, a promotional newsletter, stated:

"There is a 2,700 acre tract of wild land with a trout stream running through it for guests who want to fish or hunt."[19]

Aside from all of the many activities the Northernaire offered, fishing was still important to many of the guests.

"A 49 inch Muskie was caught off the Show Boat dock. No, we can't guarantee that you will land one this big. Yes, there are even larger ones in our lakes. It's a challenge!"[20]

Marty died at the age of eighty in 1979, a year after my parents and I joined him for wildlife films that winter day.

After Marty died, the resort passed through a series of owners, including Fred Schlagel, who worked to keep the hotel's reputation for world-class entertainment alive.

"A near sell-out crowd is expected to pack the Northernaire in Three Lakes this Saturday, August 13, for the performance of internationally known comedian Bob Hope," reported *The Three Lakes News* in 1983.[21]

Bob Hope's appearance on that sweltering August night may have marked the end of the grand resort's attempt to retain the glory of years past. The rest of the world, or at least the northwoods resort industry, was catching up to Carl Marty's vision, and by the late '80s and early '90s fancy new resorts and condominium developments were appearing on a regular basis on prime northern lakes.

The Northernaire was still in operation, but just barely it seemed, when my wife and I stopped there in the summer of 1990. We had just moved to Rhinelander, and my own memory of the Northernaire and Carl Marty on that odd winter day in 1978 prompted me to take her there one Saturday afternoon. We had hoped to eat lunch there in the big dining room but were informed that the Northernaire no longer offered lunch, just dinner.

Soon after, the grand northwoods resort was closed due to bankruptcy and stood silent and vacant overlooking Deer Lake.

In December of 1995 a corporate partnership, BarKat LLC, based in Milwaukee, purchased the property at a sheriff's foreclosure sale for $625,000.[22] The plan was to raze the old Northernaire and build an expansive new condominium development on the 1,800 feet of prime lakeshore property.

"A new lodging and restaurant complex may rise like the phoenix from the ruins of the withering old Northernaire in Three Lakes," reported Tom Michele of the *Rhinelander Daily News*.[23]

Carl Marty's dream vanished from the face of the earth as the Wisconsin northwoods eased toward summer. "The landmark Northernaire Hotel, once called the 'Waldorf of the Wilderness,' is scheduled for demolition next week, with the new owners of the property planning to build a new hotel with condominium units to replace the present structure," reported the *Rhinelander Daily News* in May of 1996.[24]

BarKat's project never materialized. After facing years of stiff opposition from local residents and landowners concerned about the size of the proposed project and possible negative impacts to the lakes, as well as the inability to gain approval from the county, BarKat abandoned the project.[25] Eventually an Eau Claire–based development group purchased the property.[26]

With new owners toting a scaled-down development plan, the phoenix did rise from the ruins of Marty's Waldorf in 2007.

"Sixty years after the original hotel and vacation complex was built, the Northernaire lives again," reported the *Rhinelander Daily News* in August.[27]

But the resort complex, now called the Northernaire Resort and Spa—which officially opened when the secretary of the Wisconsin Department of Tourism and a state senator snipped a ribbon in front of the entrance doors on an August day twenty-four years after Bob Hope entertained 3,500 people under the Northernaire's big tent and long after Rusty and Bernese walked the grounds— resembled the old resort in name only.

The original Northernaire, the product of Carl Marty's vision, had once occupied a special place in time and possessed a certain style and a unique grace that will never be duplicated.

Entrance to Long Lake Lodge Courtesy of Janet McClure

Chapter 7

Hazen's Long Lake Lodge

Something can happen when people first step into the lodge of a historic northwoods Wisconsin resort. A certain sort of feeling takes over when the old screen door creaks and slams behind them and the modern world with all of its trappings is left behind.

Maybe it's the look of hand-hewn timbers, or a ceiling of knotty pine, or the photos of generations of anglers adorning the walls.

Or maybe it is simply a sense of the people themselves, the thousands through the years that sought refuge at a quiet place on a quiet lake somewhere "north of the tension zone." The dads and granddads who told countless stories while being warmed by a fire of birch and maple logs. The endless rainy day games of dominoes packed into a weeklong vacation that never seemed to last long enough.

The feeling is strongest inside the oldest of northwoods resorts, those with origins that go back seventy-five or even one hundred years or more to when adventurous entrepreneurs followed close on the heels of the white pine loggers to begin to transform the northwoods economy from one of lumbering into one of tourism and recreation.

The Hazen Inn, located on Long Lake just east of Phelps in Vilas County, is one of those resorts. Known for more than one hundred years as Hazen's Long Lake Lodge, the Hazen Inn is one of the oldest resorts still operating in northern Wisconsin. Stepping into the inn's main lodge on a warm day recently, I could immediately feel the history of the place.

The original lodge building was built in 1900, when elsewhere in the United States John Philip Sousa was making a name for himself as a pretty good bandleader and Carrie Nation was smashing taverns in the name of temperance. In 1915, the year the millionth Ford rolled off the line, a dining area was added, and in the 1920s the lodge was expanded to include a great room centered around a black granite fireplace.

Today the resort is being run as a bed-and-breakfast inn by Joel and Janet McClure, transplanted Iowans with a flair for hospitality and a strong respect for history. The McClures purchased the century-old lodge after their son happened upon it in 1993 and they made the decision to leave their lives in Iowa to run a bed-and-breakfast resort in the northwoods. At the time they hadn't quite realized that they had just purchased an important piece of northwoods history.

"We really weren't aware of the long history of the lodge until we bought it and started learning about Charles Hazen and the Hazen family," Janet McClure told me as we sat in the original dining room of the resort under the watchful eyes of a buck and a snowy owl mounted decades before I was born. "As time went by we learned more and more."[1]

What they learned was that, as with many of the old northwoods resorts, the Long Lake Lodge began because of one man with a vision. Charles E. Hazen was born in Monroe County, New York, in 1872. At the age of sixteen, he left New York for adventure, ending up in Conover, Wisconsin, where he became employed by the Twin Lake Hunting and Fishing Club (later known as the Lakota Resort). For a number of years Hazen remained in the northwoods, working at several different resorts. At the time, entrepreneurs were first beginning to cater to the new breed of sportsman, the fellow who would pay good money for a north Wisconsin fishing or hunting experience.

Hazen liked what he saw and wanted to be a part of the developing northwoods resort industry. In order to acquire enough capital to build his own resort, he headed down to Chicago in 1895. For five years he worked for the *Drovers' Journal*, the publication for cattlemen, as the manager of a stock barn.

With money saved, Hazen returned to the northwoods in 1900 and purchased fifty-three acres on the shores of Long Lake. Using tamarack logs cut nearby and lumber he purchased in Chicago and had shipped by rail to Conover and then hauled to Long Lake, he built three log cabins in 1900 and a main lodge building in 1901. The Long Lake Lodge, originally a simple fishing camp, was born.

After the turn of the century, resorts began to offer amenities that far surpassed those of the early primitive hunting and fishing camps as the tourist base grew to include families. Hazen's resort was no exception. Fresh vegetables, eggs, cream, and milk were produced on the property. A maple syrup camp was started to provide guests with fresh syrup for breakfast. The resort was one of the first to have electricity—thanks to a fifteen-horsepower Fairbanks-Morse engine generator—and steam heat run to the cabins through an underground tunnel system.

Hazen, who became known in the area as "Uncle Charlie," continually improved and expanded the resort. Eventually the resort covered three hundred acres with one thousand feet of shoreline and included eleven tamarack log cabins. It became a classic example of the family-operated northwoods resort.

Passed down to Uncle Charlie's son, Harvey, and then to Harvey's daughter Sunny Fondrie, Hazen's Long Lake Lodge endured as a family-owned operation for more than seventy-five years—a time that could be called the golden age of the traditional northwoods resort.

The resort was sold by the Fondries in 1978 and changed hands several times in the next few years as subsequent owners failed to stay solvent. A bank foreclosure in the late 1980s resulted in many of the cabins being sold off to individuals. No longer being run as a resort, the main lodge was neglected and fell into disrepair.

Luckily, it was at this time that the old lodge somehow found the McClures. "When we purchased the lodge in 1993 it was in a state of neglect and required a lot of work," said Janet McClure. "During rainstorms or melting snow we had to place buckets in the dining room. Some of the showers leaked, and we would have guests reporting that the water was coming through the ceilings in the great room behind the sofa or chairs in which they were sitting. Cold air would rush into the inn through the openings between the logs and around the poorly insulated windows. Bats would be flying about routinely most nights . . . a challenging and exciting event!"[2]

During the first few years of ownership the McClures spent long hours making emergency repairs, and then came the effort to restore the old lodge to its original glory.

"Everything that we made the first five or more years went right back into the maintenance and repair of the structure," said Janet McClure.[3]

The McClures' hard work has paid off. The flavor and atmosphere of Charles Hazen's Long Lake Lodge has been revived and can be enjoyed by guests at what is now called the Hazen Inn. An old pine sideboard remains in the same location in the dining room as seen in resort postcards from the earliest days. The bald eagle that Uncle Charlie killed and had mounted after it attempted to snack on his live duck decoys in the early 1900s still perches inside a display case at one end of the lodge, a testament to a bygone era.

Today, most visitors to the Hazen Inn go there for the relaxation and quiet it provides, but guests soon realize that the greatest asset of the resort is its century of northwoods history.

Teal Lake Lodge, 1930 WHi Image ID 37953

Chapter 8
First Resorts:
Teal Lake Lodge

I t seems that Tim Ross was born to run a resort. Tim, who with his wife, Prudence, runs Ross' Teal Lake Lodge east of Hayward, is the third-generation Ross to own the resort. But the Ross tradition of providing hospitality goes way, way back.

"An ancestor, Major Ossian Ross, opened the first inn in Illinois territory in 1823," Ross told me as we sat in the combination home and office that overlooks Teal Lake while the four resident Labrador retrievers ambled in and out through the front door, left open to let in the unseasonably warm air. "A real character, he went on to build the first hotel and multistoried building in Illinois in 1827."[1] Abraham Lincoln was a noteworthy recipient of early Ross hospitality.

Ross descendents eventually found their way to northern Wisconsin, joining in the growing resort industry there. Tim Ross's grandfather, Walter Ross, was a partner in the Pike Lake Resort near Fifield until he decided to purchase his own resort in 1921.

He found a suitable property on Teal Lake, twenty-one miles by horse and wagon from the nearest train depot in Hayward.

The existing resort Walter Ross purchased had originated as a satellite fishing camp for Cornick's resort based on nearby Spider Lake in 1904 and consisted of a main lodge and dining room and several log cottages. The original buildings were the first permanent structures to be built on Teal Lake. The dining room and kitchen in the main lodge as well as two cottages still exist.

"It was the first resort in the area," said Ross. "Like many of the early resorts, the original owner basically 'squatted' on land owned by the logging companies."[2] Walter Ross began improving the resort, building a lounge in 1923.

A promotional brochure from that year sounds irresistible:

You are in Virgin Timber on the banks of a beautiful lake. Log cottages, clean, screened, well furnished, comfortable beds. Meals include the best of meats, also your own fish and game when wanted, fresh vegetables, fruits; cream from our own herd of cows. We have a deep well of cold drinking water. Evinrude motors can be furnished. Several well stocked Trout Streams nearby.[3]

The brochure's intended target was the typical resort guest of the day, an upper-middle-class or wealthy professional with enough money to spend on what was then considered the elite vacation.

"In the very early days the sports would come up just to fish, mostly for musky," Ross said. "The musky was the elite fish then, held in very high esteem. The clientele at that time was professional level, men with money. They would come up on the trains from Chicago or Minneapolis, and a vacation could last a month. In the 1920s and '30s they often would arrive with a whole staff, complete with chauffeur."[4]

From the early days of Teal Lake Lodge the vacation to the northwoods was a family affair, and the resort became more than just a place to catch fish. Other advantages of a northwoods vacation, such as the health benefits for allergy sufferers, were promoted as well. The 1923 brochure suggests that women and children might enjoy picking wild berries.

The only way to get to Teal Lake for many years was by railroad—the Minneapolis, St. Paul and Sault Ste. Marie (better known simply as the Soo)—to Stone Lake and then by horse and wagon to the resort. Ross's grandfather improved on the situation by acquiring one of the first automobiles in the area, which could transport guests while the wagon team followed behind with gear and supplies.

"Our auto will meet you and you will find the drive of twenty-three miles over excellent roads a real pleasure," stated the 1923 brochure.

Ross holds his share of personal memories of Teal Lake.

"Until I was eight years old I just spent the summers there," said Ross. "As a kid I remember getting on the train in Chicago where we lived and falling asleep, and waking up in a bed at the resort. Then in 1948 Dad took over the resort and we moved there."[5]

Ross fondly remembers the resort's fishing guides: "We had five guides, two that guided for crappies and walleye, and the rest strictly musky. They lived right at the resort in the guides' shack during the season; in the winter they did other things. Most of the guides were old lumberjacks, in their sixties and seventies when I was a kid. They had known the resort from the early days."[6]

Ross learned to fish from legendary area guides such as the Metcalf brothers and Emory "Muskrat" Turnbell and his son Bud. All are gone now, except for Bud Turnbell, who is in his eighties and still lives in the area. Two Teal Lake guides, Paul Quail and Ken Eck, are now memorialized in the Freshwater Fishing Hall of Fame in Hayward.

"I used a Pflueger Supreme reel," Ross said. "That's what I grew up with. I put myself through college by guiding in the summers."

Guides continued to reside at the resort until the 1960s. "With better transportation in the area, the guides began to live at home with their families," said Ross. However, even today the resort is happy to book a guide for guests.

Tim Ross left the resort to attend prep school and then college. A stint in the army and other employment followed, but he returned in 1978 to take the Teal Lake reins over from his father, Nelson Ross.

As each generation had done before him, he has adapted to the times and made some changes. A big outdoor swimming pool came first. An eighteen-hole golf course was added in the early 1990s.

Despite all the changes made through the years, the flavor of the original resort remains strong. Guests still use parts of the main lodge and dining areas built in 1907. Also, two of the original cabins from 1907 remain on the property. One can accommodate fourteen people. "That cabin is still used by guests," said Ross. "It's one of our most popular cabins."

"Tradition is more than important to us, it's vital," said Ross. "It is our way of life, what we do." The Ross tradition at Teal Lake is secured for the future, as the Ross's daughter Victoria, the fourth generation, is actively involved with management of the resort.

Buying duck decoys WHi Image ID 40785

Chapter 9
Mel's Trading Post

Walking through the doors of Mel's Trading Post, a sporting goods store located at the south end of Rhinelander's downtown district, is like taking a step back to a simpler time. There are none of the bright lighting and endless racks of mass-produced merchandise of the discount chain stores. You won't find rows of cash registers or overhead security cameras. What you will find is a tremendous variety of quality outdoor gear packed into two floors of a historic building, what was once the original Rhinelander Montgomery Ward store. You'll also find salespeople who know what they are talking about and are committed to helping you find just what you need. Whether it be duck decoys and rigging, wool shirts and pants, rifles, scopes, and cartridges, Mel's most likely has what you are looking for.

The store's origins go back to the late 1940s. "Dad started with the store in 1946," said Mitch Mode, one of Mel Mode's five children and current store owner. "He was a good baseball player and actually had a contract with the Chicago Cubs. He seemed well on the way to a baseball career, but a back injury put the skids on that plan."[1]

Mode returned to his hometown of Rhinelander and jumped into business with friend Del Stengl, who operated a variety store on Brown Street called the Trading Post. The store carried "the most varied supply of sporting goods in northern Wisconsin," but also appliances, televisions, and souvenirs. The Trading Post was a great stop for tourists due to the Norway pine trees that added a north-woods touch to the store interior. The trees were created with mortar-covered steel columns as trunks and real pine boughs, which were replaced twice a year.

In the early 1960s Mode acquired the entire business from his partner and moved the store into its current location, Rhinelander's old Woolworth Building. Now known as Mel's Trading Post, the store continued to offer a diverse mix of merchandise but no longer sold appliances or electronics. Concentrating more on hunting and fishing gear, Mode also took advantage of ever-changing recreational trends. "Dad was a big skier and began to offer downhill gear as skiing became popular in the 1960s," recalled Mitch. "He also had a Honda motorcycle business for a time and got into cross-country skiing equipment when that sport exploded in popularity in the 1970s."

Although the Trading Post's core through the years has always been hunting and fishing gear, the "golden age" of deer hunter activity at the store was back in the 1950s and '60s. Mitch fondly remembers those days when the store was a magnet for hunters on the Friday before opening day of the gun season.

Before the time when hunters could purchase their licenses and permits early, a great influx of hunters would descend upon the store the Friday before Saturday's opener—to purchase licenses and party permits and to stock up on last-minute supplies.

"It was like a circus," Mitch recalled. "It was a very special day of the year, almost like Christmas. We'd have a line of hunters fifteen to twenty deep waiting to buy licenses and the store would be wall-to-wall people. In those days there was no blaze orange requirement, and everyone in the store would be wearing red wool. My sister would drive home from college just to be there for that day, it was such an exciting day." The store would fill with local hunters and their friends and relatives from out of the area, as well as out-of-state hunters. "Since the season had yet to begin everyone was in a festive and happy mood," said Mitch.

In the times before the blaze orange requirement and hunter safety training, hunting accidents and fatalities were much more frequent. In small towns across the north, insurance companies offered short-term "deer hunter policies," life insurance just in case the hunter was a victim of a fatal accident. "At the Trading Post, Dad would set up a card table right in the store for agents to sell insurance to hunters," said Mitch. "He would alternate between the two agents in town each year."

After the season opened, a Mode family tradition was to visit the old Hotel Fenlon down the street to see what deer were currently hanging on the meat pole erected in front of the hotel. In those days every business in town benefited from the deer season and catered to hunters for nine days. The hotels were packed with hunters, cafés and restaurants promoted hunter specials, and special church services were held for hunters.

"Although deer season is still a very big thing, deer hunting had a much bigger impact in those days than it does today," said Mode. "Customers to the store are more spread out now, buying licenses and gear early, although there is still an increase in business just prior to the opener."

Mel Mode loved to hunt and fish, particularly duck hunting up on Lac Vieux Desert, but he had little time for these pursuits—the downside to owning a sporting goods store.

"When Dad was building the business he worked long days, seven days a week. There was just no time to do anything else," said Mitch. "One time someone lifted a fishing reel and pretty much eliminated Dad's profits for the week." A tireless worker, Mode loved to be in the store—there was no drudgery about it for him.

While growing up, the Mode kids also put in their time. "The first job I remember that I actually got paid for was when I was seven years old," recalled Mitch. "Dad had purchased boxes of fishing lures on some closeout. They were all jumbled up in big cardboard boxes. I sorted them out one by one and received a penny apiece for my efforts."

All of the five Mode kids worked at the store as time allowed. "During the summer we were all there," said Mitch. "When I was junior high age I remember Dad would wheel a popcorn machine in front of the store and for seventy-five cents an hour I would sell popcorn."

The summer months also brought in the fishermen. "In those days people came up to the northwoods to fish; fishing was the real focus for family vacations," said Mitch. "Customers would bring to the store the big fish they had taken out on the lakes. Dad had made a box with a glass front that fish could be displayed in. It was cooled with ice and placed outside the front of the store. There was always someone's prize musky or walleye on display. Sometimes a fisherman would call at one or two in the morning, wanting dad to put a fish in the box. It was a big thing."

Mel's has changed through the years, but it still retains the flavor and atmosphere of an old-time sporting goods store. There is an enormous variety of items on the shelves and racks, although nothing in great quantity. But more times than not you can find what you are looking for.

Although Rhinelander has experienced an influx of discount chain stores, the family-operated Trading Post has been able to survive through the years by fostering an exceptionally strong customer base, from younger people buying snowboarding gear to the die-hard waterfowlers, deer hunters, and anglers.

"Our key is our people. We have the local expertise, experts in duck hunting, fly-fishing, firearms, skiing, and camping. They know the area and offer more than just ringing up a sale," said Mode. "While the big stores can hurt business, we aren't so much competing against them as we are competing for people's discretionary funds, the limited amount of money they have to spend on recreation or entertainment. There are just a lot more things for people to spend their money on these days."

Another key to the continuing success of Mel's Trading Post is the quality of items sold at the store. "I don't sell cheap stuff," said Mitch. "I want high quality, but at a reasonable price. I don't want a person coming back with something that is broken or defective. I want satisfied customers."

This combination of exceptional customer service and a diverse line of products has kept Mel's Trading Post going strong for more than sixty years. When you step into the store and the old original wood floorboards creak underneath your feet, and you scan the racks of wool and flannel shirts, rifles, and duck decoys, you know you've found a piece of hunting and fishing tradition.

Pastika's Sport Shop Courtesy of Leon Pastika

Chapter 10
Pastika's Sport Shop: Ninety Years of Muskies and Minnows

Leon Pastika was a high school student in the fall of 1949, more interested in chasing girls than keeping track of the trophy fish that successful anglers frequently brought to his father Charlie's bait shop in downtown Hayward. The fishermen most likely had bought their bait at the shop, and when they caught big fish on the waters of the nearby Chippewa Flowage the shop was the natural place to do a little showing off.

However, in October of that year a local tavern owner and die-hard musky fisherman came into town with a catch from the flowage that no one could ignore, not even a distracted teenager. Louis Spray had landed the big one, a nearly seventy-pound national-record-breaking behemoth that immediately became known simply as the "Spray musky."

"I remember when he caught the musky," Leon told me. "He drug it all over town showing people, had it down at Stone Lake and weighed at the post office there."[1]

The Spray musky really put the little northwoods town of Hayward on the map. Although the region had long been recognized in the Upper Midwest for the incredible fishing opportunities found on the Chippewa Flowage, or "Big Chip," and surrounding lakes, the record-breaking fish brought national attention. Through the years the legend and lore of the Spray musky became a part of Hayward itself. Forever intertwined with the story of the fabled fish is the story of Pastika's Sport Shop.

The origins of Pastika's, perhaps the oldest continuously operating bait and tackle store in Wisconsin, go back to 1921.

"My dad moved up here from Rice Lake right after WWI in 1919 as a harness maker," said Leon Pastika, now seventy-six years old. "The gentleman he worked for died and Dad took over the business, but shortly after the harness business went to hell! Cars replaced horses. So in 1921 my mother and father started a dry goods business, selling clothing and also souvenirs for the tourists. There was a very small fishing tackle supply, a few fish hooks and things."[2]

The new shop did pretty well until the Great Depression found its way to northwest Wisconsin in the early 1930s. Pastika said:

When the Depression came along everything went to pot. Dad worked for WPA, but we had a bait shop, too, and Dad hung in there, moving to different locations around Hayward. Even during the Depression we did well on the bait business. The resort business was strong; people with money were still coming up north. They would come up for two or three weeks or even a month for vacation. Each resort had fishing guides hired. Most of the guides in the area were working out of the resorts, making about three to five dollars a week then. The guides would come in for bait, and sometimes the tourists came in to buy their own bait. We had the same group coming in every year from the Chicago Fishing Club out on Lac Courte Oreilles which began back in the 1920s.[3]

After WWII the economy got better and the bait store began to grow and we moved locations. By this time I was in high school and helped Dad out. My brother and I both worked at the shop.

I remember back in the 1940s we used to ship a lot of fish out. We'd put the tourists' fish on ice and ship them out of the Soo Line station at Stone Lake. They'd go to Milwaukee and Chicago and other places.[4]

Eventually the shop ended up at the corner currently occupied by the Kwik Trip convenience store:

We converted a tire store into a bait shop. This location was kitty-corner to the Moccasin Bar owned by Louis Spray, so Dad and Louie talked a lot. My dad knew Louis well. We were still mostly a bait shop, just live bait, minnows, and night crawlers. Our tackle supply was really just three or four muffin tins filled with hooks, minnow pails, and a few cane poles. Even up into the early 1950s all we'd carry was two types of flathead spoons, Dardevles, Pikie Minnows, Surf-Orenos, and Pflueger Globes—that covered about 90 percent of the tackle.[5]

In 1947 Pastika's moved to the location where the shop still stands, along Highway 27 a little south of downtown.

"Through the 1940s and 1950s people still came up to Hayward for two weeks or more," said Pastika. "I remember when it began to drop down to a week, and then to three- or four-day weekends."

In 1955 Charlie Pastika retired and Leon bought the shop. After running the store for more than four decades, Leon suffered a heart attack and decided it was time to retire. In 1998 he put the store up for sale. Fortunately for Pastika and Hayward, a buyer came along who would be just as committed to Pastika's Sport Shop as Leon had been.

Al and Sue Rosenquist had been going to Hayward for fishing vacations for many years and were in love with the area. The Rosenquists, originally from northern Illinois, had set a goal for themselves that after their wedding they would permanently move to Hayward within five years. Buying Pastika's was a perfect way to fulfill that goal.

"I had a friend who wanted to invest in a business in the area and asked me if I knew of anything. I didn't but then I noticed that Pastika's was for sale," Al Rosenquist told me. "I told my friend about it, but he decided he wasn't interested in running a bait and tackle store. Then I realized that it was something we could do, so we bought it."[6]

The Rosenquists immediately appreciated the shop's place in Hayward history, but they did decide to take some aspects of the business in new directions.

"The biggest move we made was to increase the musky end of things," said Rosenquist. "That part of the store was a little light, and I'm a big musky fisherman. Through the years we've evolved into a musky store, but we do have everything else as well; we've increased the stock all around."

Although a new direction for the shop, the expansion toward more musky gear is highly appropriate considering Pastika's Sport Shop's place in musky fishing lore.

Also, the specialization was actually just the thing to keep the seventy-five-year-old store competitive in a world of superstores and cheap imports. Sales have grown dramatically since the Rosenquists took over, primarily due to the development of the musky store with a mail-order component.

"We do an incredible amount of business through the catalog," said Rosenquist. "The catalog just happened by accident. We started a Web site and people kept asking us when we would start a catalog—there weren't many musky catalogs out there, and people wanted another option. We said if we're going to do this we'll do it right and jumped right into it. It's been highly successful."

When walk-in business is slow in the winter, it's the catalog business that gets them through, according to Rosenquist.

Despite catalogs and Web sites, the shop started by Charlie Pastika in 1921 is still a big draw for tourists in the area, a "must-stop" destination because of its history.

"Forty-five-year-old dads will look at the fish pool and tell me they have a picture of themselves in front of the pool when they were five years old," said Rosenquist. "The history of the place draws people."

To this day a photo of Louis Spray and the musky, inscribed to Charlie Pastika, hangs in the store, a reminder to all who enter of the long and rich history of Pastika's Sport Shop.

Duke Montgomery in his shop Courtesy of Jim Montgomery

Chapter 11
Duke's Outboards:
A Northwoods Institution

For more than sixty years in the north-central Wisconsin lakes country of Vilas and Oneida counties, if someone had an outboard motor in need of repair, there was no question of where to take it—Duke's Outboards. While the business is now run by Duke's son in a new location, fans of antique outboards can still get a feel for the old shop at Rhinelander's Duke Montgomery Antique Outboard Motor and Boat Museum.

Duke Montgomery's shop was easy to find—you just needed to follow the white directional signs from the main highway to the Wisconsin River just north of Rhinelander—and anyone could tell you that if you brought your outboard to Duke Montgomery it would be fixed, and fixed right.

Vernon "Duke" Montgomery was just nineteen years old and a recent high school graduate when he started his Evinrude dealership and outboard repair business in the midst of the Great Depression in 1934. It had been only five years earlier when Ole Evinrude's family-owned company, Elto (Evinrude Light Twin Outboards), had merged with the original Evinrude company (which Ole had sold in 1914) to eventually form the Outboard Motors Corporation (OMC).[1] In spite of poor economic times, Ole Evinrude developed two new outboards in 1934, and sales weren't bad by Depression-era standards.[2]

Originally located behind his father's café in the old Commercial Hotel in Rhinelander, Duke's business was one of the first Evinrude dealerships in the area, and he sold and repaired outboards for northwoods residents and the thousands of visitors to the area until poor health forced him to retire in 1999.

I recently had the opportunity to visit with Duke and his wife, Dorothy. Though age and poor hearing has made it difficult for Duke to communicate these days, his passion for outboards was communicated by his smile and shining eyes as he quietly told me about the early days.

The original shop was on Brown Street in downtown Rhinelander, Duke said. He smiled as he told me about throwing a small Evinrude over his shoulder and walking up and down Brown Street with it to promote his shop and the Evinrude product. "It was something different," he said. "I was setting the trap and when people asked about it the trap was sprung."[3]

After two years at the Brown Street location, Duke moved the shop to a location north of town on the Wisconsin River's Boom Lake, where he would have water access. It was there that Duke's Outboards became a northwoods institution.

While Duke was gaining a reputation as an expert outboard mechanic, he also had a "day job."

"Duke worked the graveyard shift at the Rhinelander paper mill," Dorothy said. "He'd come home from work and immediately begin working on the outboards. He'd work all weekend too. People would come from a fifty-mile radius to bring their motors to Duke, and he put in very long hours to meet the demand."[4]

After taking an early retirement from the paper mill in the mid-1970s, Duke began to devote all his time to the outboard business.

Duke was witness to the development of a major American industry.

"In the early years there was no real market for outboards," Duke said. "Outboards were used only for practical purposes, just by fishermen or duck hunters. The market didn't take off until there was something the public was really looking for."

According to Duke, this "something" was the development of shrouded, or covered, motors. The two outboard models introduced by Ole Evinrude in 1934—the Imperial versions of the 5.5-horsepower Lightwin and the 9.2-horsepower Lightfour—were the first truly shrouded outboards.[5]

"This simply made the outboards look nicer," Duke said. "People liked that."

In the 1960s Duke expanded his business to include snowmobile sales and repair, taking advantage of the increasing popularity of the sport. However, by the mid-1970s he dropped the snowmobile business, finding they were too much of a headache with frequent breakdowns.[6]

Through the years Duke worked on just about every type of American outboard made, and few knew an outboard motor as well as Duke did.

After having seen and repaired too many motors to ever count, Duke did mention he had a favorite Evinrude model.

"One of my favorites was the four-cylinder, 5.4-horsepower Zephyr," Duke said. "This had a nice running engine. It was made between 1940 and 1960."

After devoting sixty-five years to the outboard motor business, age finally caught up with Duke and forced him to completely retire in 1999. Duke and Dorothy's son, Jim Montgomery, who had learned the outboard business from his father, came back from Alaska (where he had been living for twenty years) to take over the business from Duke. Jim carries on the Duke's Outboards tradition of quality service from a new shop located not far from Duke's original Boom Lake shop. A reminder of Duke's legacy is an incredible collection of antique outboard motors.

From the early days of his shop, Duke began collecting outboards—generally those left for repairs and never picked up. Eventually there came to be more than a hundred outboards in the collection, one of the most diverse antique outboard motor collections in Wisconsin. Jim Montgomery began to display several of his dad's motors—representatives of different makes and models—at his shop, and he also began collecting antique outboards himself.

"People would come into my shop and be just fascinated with the old motors, but there were many more of my dad's outboards in storage. I didn't have space to display all of them," said Montgomery. "I thought they should be put on display in a museum setting for people to enjoy."[7]

As a tribute to Duke and the Wisconsin outboard industry, Jim Montgomery spearheaded an effort to establish the Duke Montgomery Antique Outboard Motor and Boat Museum in Rhinelander. Duke's outboard collection is the core of the museum, which was established in 2005 and is housed in the Pioneer Historical Park along with a logging museum and a railroad museum.

On display are pre-1960 outboard motors as well as historic wooden boats manufactured in Wisconsin, antique fishing equipment, and a recreation of Duke Montgomery's old shop.

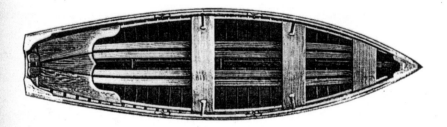

MODEL NO. 60

Length	14 ft.	Depth Amidship	16 in.
Beam	44 in.	Depth at Stern	20 in.
Depth at Bow	24 in.	Seats	4

Approximate weight ----------- 150 lbs.

Our 14 ft. Smooth Planked Row Boat

THIS boat was designed for easy rowing and for this reason it has always been a favorite among resort owners. It has a sturdy White Oak frame and is smooth planked with Cedar. All fastenings are galvanized, the rowlock sockets of malleable iron are cast from our own patterns, machined to fit and bolted on to stay.

The smooth planked construction makes it easier to repair, and easier to keep clean. Your choice of pin or loose oarlocks.

Price, with one pair of first grade oars -- $65.00

RHINELANDER BOAT CO.

RHINELANDER   PHONE 157   **WISCONSIN**

We reserve the right to alter prices without notice.

"The Scout," a Rhinelander Boat Company mainstay Courtesy of Joy Vancos

Chapter 12
The Rhinelander Boat Company

T he early 1900s saw the development of the sports enthusiast. Americans had progressed from the subsistence homestead lifestyle, where hunting and fishing were necessities rather than recreational pursuits, to a more automated society where goods and services, including food, could be purchased with cash at the market. People were discovering the idea of leisure time, and a good economy put some extra cash in their pockets. Those with sporting interests were spending money and time on hunting and fishing trips, and they were buying manufactured sporting goods—deer rifles, shotguns, fishing rods, and boats.

Wisconsin has a rich history of sporting equipment manufacturers. Perhaps the pinnacle of the early manufacturers of sporting equipment were the companies that produced exceptionally high quality wooden fishing and pleasure boats during the first half of the twentieth century. The north-central Wisconsin lakes country was home to several enterprises that produced quality wooden boats, the names of many of them largely unknown to the modern-day sportsman.

For collectors or lovers of these boats, those produced by the Rhinelander Boat Company (RBC) hold a special place in their hearts, and those that may own these classic boats guard them jealously.

Some form of the RBC existed from 1903 through the early 1950s. The company-produced rowboats were generally constructed with a white oak frame with cedar planking and distinctive redwood seats. The flat-bottomed "Fisherman" model weighed about 165 pounds and sold for thirty-six dollars in 1934. Fishermen, resort owners, and summer camps purchased RBC boats for half a century. The company also produced beautiful canvas-covered cedar canoes.

There are several chapters to the history of the RBC, much of it unwritten and lost to the years. However, Rhinelander resident Joy Vancos was able to piece together the early history of the company. A local historian with a family interest in early wooden boats—her husband's family owned an RBC boat—Vancos searched old newspapers, land records, and obituaries to compile the little-known story of the birth of the Rhinelander Boat Company.

"Many believe the history of the Rhinelander Boat Company began with the business established by William Cleveland on Ocala Street in Rhinelander in 1910," said Vancos. "Actually, Cleveland's business is only the second part of the story."[1]

"The original Rhinelander Boat Company was founded by Frank Sayner in 1903," said Vancos. "Sayner was already involved in the boat building business in Vilas County when he purchased property between Kemp Street and the Pelican River in Rhinelander, where he built a three-story boat factory."[2]

Interestingly, Frank Sayner was the brother of Orrin Sayner for whom the Vilas County town of Sayner was named. A railroad depot was established on property owned by Orrin Sayner, and the depot was given his name. Sayner established a well-known resort on the shores of Plum Lake.

"Frank Sayner specialized in rowboats and launches," said Vancos. "The new company enjoyed an extremely good business."[3]

Many of the notable residents of Rhinelander purchased custom-made RBC boats. According to Vancos, the most spectacular vessel was the one built for Gene Shepard, the man who would go down in northwoods history as the creator of Rhinelander's mythical forest-dwelling beast, the Hodag. "The boat was sixty-one feet overall with an eleven-foot beam. It was described as being powered by a thirty-horsepower engine and having two cabins, along with a kitchen and pantry, toilet, and bath," said Vancos.

"Unfortunately, a fire destroyed the boat factory building in 1905," said Vancos. "For two months stockholders pondered the future of the company but finally decided to reorganize and rebuild. The new factory was considerably different from the old one. Buildings were arranged at ground level only and separated from each other."[4]

Despite the reorganization, the business affairs of the company began to founder, and Frank Sayner apparently left the scene in 1908.

"In October of 1908 it was announced that the remaining stock of boats would be sold and the business would close," said Vancos. "An attempt to reopen the company in the spring of 1909 failed, and the factory was closed permanently in 1910."

The Rhinelander Boat Company

According to Vancos, William Cleveland, a former employee of the now-defunct company, began building his own wooden boats in 1910 and called his new business the Rhinelander Boat Company.

A Rhinelander newspaper, *The New North*, ran a story about Cleveland's company in 1911, whose name was changed to the Oneida Boat Company shortly after its founding:

> The plant of the Oneida Boat Company in this city is now in operation and prospects are that it will keep busy throughout the winter and well into the spring. W. E. Cleveland, who is the manager and chief owner of the factory, stated, Monday, that the company has a large number of orders on hand which will necessitate the employment of at least half a dozen workmen for many months to come.
>
> The plant is located on the south side, one block west of the brewery. It is equipped with all machinery for the manufacture of high-grade rowboats, canoes, and launches. Gasoline engine and motor repairing is also one of the specialties of the concern.[5]

The reborn RBC produced boats until the early 1950s, when lightweight, low-maintenance aluminum boats took over the boating market. Today the old, finely crafted wooden boats are prized by collectors and may sometimes be found at antique boat shows.

Wisconsin market hunters, 1903 Courtesy of the Oshkosh Public Museum

Chapter 13
Waterfowl Hunting
with Live Decoys

T he severe drought that much of America experienced in the early 1930s was a major factor in the agricultural disaster of the dust bowl and was also devastating to waterfowl populations as once-productive wetlands dried up. Plummeting duck numbers led to more restrictive hunting regulations. One common practice of both the market and recreational waterfowl hunter that was regulated out of existence in 1935 was the use of live decoys.

The use of live decoys in waterfowling was a practice brought to America by European colonists. The use of "stool birds" to lure an unsuspecting flock to the gun was certainly used by early colonists, but the method gained in popularity as large-scale market hunting developed in the East and Midwest after the Civil War.[1]

On the East Coast live decoys were used primarily in goose hunting. The Outdoor Life book *The Story of American Hunting and Firearms* described the use of live decoys for goose hunting on the sand spits of bays around Long Island:

> A decoy rig consisted of between fifteen and forty geese of both sexes, taken to the spit in coops. Stakes were driven into the sand at regular intervals and a bird was tethered to each stake by a leather leg strap or hobble. The most valuable member of the rig (worth up to two hundred dollars) was a trained gander tethered some distance from the other birds, so that its calls would attract wild geese passing overhead.
>
> . . . [T]he art of decoying geese reached its height of deadly efficiency along the New England coast, where the stool birds were trained—with corn and endless patience—to fly out to meet flocks of wild kin and lure them to the blinds.[2]

In Wisconsin and other Midwestern states live decoys were used for both goose and duck hunting during the late 1800s up to 1935. Many sportsmen kept a collection of mallards to be used as "live callers." While a hunter would still have a set of artificial decoys or "blocks" to provide the visual enticement, the primary purpose of the live duck was for calling.

The Wisconsin outdoor writer Gordon MacQuarrie, who wrote in the 1930s and '40s, immortalized the use of live decoys in his story "Minnie the Moocher," a tale of a pair of mallards he collected at a farm near Frederic, Wisconsin, to be used as live decoys for waterfowling. The pair, Minnie and Bill, were quite the characters. Min became a deadly caller to every passing male mallard. Bill was known for growling.[3]

MacQuarrie's story offers a glimpse into the days when live decoys were allowed in duck and goose hunting. Measured by the sporting standards of today, the use of live decoys, which could be extremely effective, may seem unsportsmanlike. When utilized by market hunters in combination with other methods such as baiting, punt guns, and sink boats to take hundreds and sometimes thousands of birds a day, the practice was indeed unfair. However, for ethical sportsmen such as MacQuarrie and many others, live decoys were an accepted tool prior to 1935.

As with MacQuarrie's Min, the mallard hen was most popular for duck hunting, while both male and female geese worked equally well as goose callers.

Sportsmen at that time cared for their live callers almost as much as they cared for their hunting dogs. A good caller might be sold for two hundred dollars or more. According to *The Story of American Hunting and Firearms*: "The man who owned a drake and half a dozen Suzies often grew as fond of them as his dog, and was thrilled to watch them lure their wild relatives down to the guns."[4]

In addition to MacQuarrie's story there are some other bits and pieces that record the nearly lost history of live decoys, with a great record coming from Wisconsin. Phillip S. Habermann, a noted Madison attorney who passed away at the age of eighty-nine in 2002, describes in his 1988 recollections duck hunting with live decoys in the 1920s: "Using live decoys, or call ducks as they were known, was a heartwarming experience that doubled the pleasure of hunting. The ways and means of how it was done should be preserved as part of our folklore."[5]

Habermann, born in 1913, was a native of Lodi and grew up near the banks of Lake Wisconsin, an impoundment on the Wisconsin River in Columbia County. Lake Wisconsin was created the year he was born, and the lake attracted "fantastic concentrations" of ducks among the dead and half-submerged trees.

"My father was an ardent duck and goose hunter from 1895 on," Habermann wrote. "Beginning before WWI he raised more than 100 mallards and six to ten Canada geese each year. The original stock for this flock came from wild birds that were wingshot. This flock furnished our live decoys."

As each autumn's waterfowl season approached, Habermann and his father would scrutinize the flock and pick out the best prospects. "There was a great difference in the talkativeness of the hen ducks," he wrote.

About half a dozen hens were chosen. Some had proved themselves the year before, while some were rookies. The chosen ducks would stay in a separate pen, except during the hunt, until the season's end.

There was a science involved in the tethering of live decoys. "To tether a live decoy while hunting it was essential to have a means of attaching a cord and weight to the duck's leg in such a manner that it would not harm the duck, and with a device that could remain in place all fall," Habermann wrote.

A half-foot-long, thin, oiled leather strap with two slots at one end and a metal D ring at the other end was part of the rig used. "You wrapped the strap around the duck's leg, inserted the slotted end through the second slot, then threaded the D ring end through the first slot and pulled it tight. The strap was locked in place until unthreaded, but could only pull around the leg loosely."

When hunting, the hunter attached a heavy chalk line to a five-pound weight and snapped the other end to the D ring on the duck's tether. The duck had a six- to ten-foot circle to paddle freely about. Some hunters placed little metal platforms, or stools, in the water for the live decoys to rest on.

Just as with the art involved in placing conventional decoys, there was an art to placing the live callers.

"The secret in placing the call ducks was to spot them where they could not see one another. Usually one went out front near the blocks and one back on either side of the blind. Being unable to see each other they became lonesome and talked back and forth, as well as calling loud and long at almost everything that flew past."

Habermann also saw the similarity between the enjoyment of watching the live decoys do their job and watching a prized dog work. "Watching and listening to the decoys work was akin to the pleasure of hunting with a fine dog," he wrote. "One never felt alone when the callers were out. You learned to understand duck talk, and could usually tell what was going on by the tone of the calls being made."

When the practice was banned, many hunters, Habermann included, lamented the end of live decoy use. "Those days are gone forever," he wrote. "But the memories and a few pictures remain. That era of our hunting history should never be forgotten."

And thanks to MacQuarrie and Habermann, it won't be.

Duck hunters and their bag Courtesy of the Oshkosh Public Museum

Chapter 14
Spring Duck Hunting
in the 1800s

T hose of us fascinated by the history of hunting and fishing in Wisconsin owe a debt of gratitude to the sportsmen of yesteryear who diligently kept records of their activities. It was a relatively common thing to keep logs or journals of activities at the deer camp, and some well-known historical deer camp journals exist. They provide important insights into attitudes and hunting methods of seasons long past. The tradition of the deer camp itself—the desire to keep track of numbers and size of animals killed—provided a powerful incentive for journal keeping.

Not very common were journals of other sporting or hunting activities. And this is why the journals kept by Louis McLane Hobbins in the late 1800s and early 1900s are unique. Hobbins was an incredibly passionate waterfowler from the Madison area, and his hunting logs provide details of every duck and goose he and his primary hunting partner, his cousin Russell "Jack" Jackson, killed.[1]

Aside from chronicling early waterfowl hunting, some other aspects of Hobbins's journals set them apart from others. Hobbins began his journals at the age of thirteen and continued them for more than twenty years. The nature of the era and bygone traditions such as spring waterfowling are recorded in them.

Hobbins's and Jackson's hunting grounds were the duck- and goose-rich marshes of the Madison chain of lakes around the dawn of the twentieth century. Hobbins's journals began in 1888 and went through 1912. Hunting ended for the year when winter blizzards and iced lakes terminated the autumn hunts, but it began anew as the lakes began to thaw.

February always found Hobbins making scouting trips to the "shanty" (probably on Lake Mendota) to search for the first arrivals of geese or ducks. Lots of ice and few birds were usually what greeted him there.

When the weather finally cooperated, hunting began in earnest in March and continued though April up to the end of the Wisconsin spring waterfowl season, generally early May.

The anticipation of a springtime waterfowl hunt is something foreign to today's sports enthusiast, whose ethics and the law dictate waterfowling be done in the fall of the year. However, Hobbins began waterfowl hunting at a time in American history when there were few regulations regarding the taking of wildlife. Although Hobbins was a recreational hunter, his era was that of the market hunter, the man who used any means possible to kill wildlife, including ducks and geese, to be sold for profit.

The excesses of market hunting began to take their toll on waterfowl numbers by the early 1900s. The Lacey Act of 1900, which banned the interstate shipment of game taken illegally, was targeted at the market hunter. However, it was the Weeks-McLean Act that really set the stage for effective waterfowl hunting regulations, including the end of springtime hunting. This law, which became effective in March 1913, gave authority to the federal government to protect and manage migratory birds.

Although Hobbins diligently made entries for every day afield, the entries typically weren't lengthy—usually just brief comments about the weather, the number of birds in the air, and the take by species.

The entry for April 19, 1897 reads:

Wind started in the morning out of the S.E. then S.W. and swung around to North with snow. Best duck weather of the season but *no birds*. All have gone north. Only got 11 bluebill.

However brief, Hobbins's entries provide a wealth of insight into the past glory days of duck hunting in Dane County. The perception of "no birds" even after bagging eleven ducks—near twice the average yearly bag of today's Wisconsin duck hunter—tells volumes about waterfowl numbers of the time.

Hobbins was as organized and accurate as he was diligent. He organized one volume of his journals into categories, providing a table of contents of sorts. Each spring and fall season was indexed with the journal page provided, as were "accidents" and "red letter days."

The red-letter days, fourteen of them over the course of eleven seasons covered by one journal, were the hunts that really stood out in Hobbins's mind because of perfect duck weather, high numbers of birds flying, and numbers taken. The red-letter days provide a real glimpse of the era.

Bird takes include those shot by both Hobbins and Jackson, as the two formed a hunting "partnership" on March 1, 1892, when Hobbins was seventeen years old:

Red-letter day, April 17, 1892:
Good shooting. 65 bluebill, 1 butterball and 1 winterduck.

Red-letter days, April 1–6, 1894:
Was good cold duck weather. We only shot 3 days and got 113 ducks mostly pintail, widgeon with a hen redhead, canvasback, bluewing teal and mallard. Could have killed hundreds of mallards but would not shoot being the marsh was simply alive with them.

Red-letter day, April 8, 1895:
We had a good day April 8th. Rainy cold day with howling north wind. Shot from 11:30 till about 12:30 and got 62 then quit on account of the rain. The next morning there was not a bird around.

Red-letter day, April 10, 1897:
A regular old duck day. Wind N. East shifting to S. East South with snow and sleet. We got 77 bluebill. This beats our record ducks in a day by 2. If we had stayed in our blinds all day we could have gotten a hundred but I have been sick and we had to go back to the cabin for something to eat.

While Hobbins and Jackson didn't hunt every day of the spring season, the pattern of Hobbins's journal entries show they probably did hunt every day they could get free during the season, but mostly around the weekends. During the season of the spring of 1892 they hunted seven days from April 11 to May 7 and totaled 254 ducks. This season included the one red-letter day when 67 ducks were taken. On another day 36 bluebill were taken.

From time to time Hobbins would provide a detailed cost accounting of his waterfowling pursuits. For the spring season of 1892 he reported total expenses to be: "Shot $2.08, Powder $2.10, Shells $2.40, Wads $1.20."

So in the spring of 1892, during a waterfowl season that lasted from March 1 to May 1 in which Hobbins and Jackson killed 254 ducks, Hobbins's total expenses were $7.78. It was money well spent to be sure.

The journal table of contents entries for "accidents" references four pages. Of the four accidents documented in the journal, three involved mishaps with boats in cold water during fall hunting seasons.

For example, the entry on November 7, 1892, reads, "Russell and myself capsized in my hunting boat lost 300 shells and had to dive for our guns in 5 feet of ice cold water then had to row 5 miles to the farmhouse with waves going right over us that was about the worst we have had yet but sporting life is hell."

Hobbins and Jackson were never the worse for the accidents, but a brief entry in October of 1892 referred to something deadly serious:

1 bluebill. The gentleman who went with me shot himself at 11:30 am and died at 6:15 pm. This is the last time that Russell and myself take anybody shooting with us.

The clipping from a Madison newspaper taped to the next two pages of the journal gave the details:

A very sad accident occurred on the north shore of Lake Mendota yesterday, and as a result the dead body of Ralph G. Cole, a student in the state university, now lies in a room at the state hospital.

The October 8, 1892, newspaper account went on to report how Cole had taken the train to Mendota Station along with Hobbins on Friday evening, and Cole, Hobbins, Jackson, and some other friends had duck hunted the following morning. Cole had left the party to pack up for a return to Madison before noon. He had returned to the farmhouse of Hans Brickson on the lakeshore and had pulled his shotgun out of the boat by its muzzle. The trigger caught on the runner of a hand sled placed in the boat for a seat, and it fired into Cole's abdomen, mortally wounding the college student.

Hobbins and Jackson were still hunting on the lake when the accident occurred, but they were quickly summoned to the farmhouse. Word of the accident soon reached Madison by telegraph, and school friends of Cole's as well as several doctors boarded the next train for Mendota Station. Despite the doctors' best efforts, Cole passed away in the early evening with Hobbins at his side.

"Louie, I am going, good-bye," were his last words.

The spring duck season was closed in Wisconsin from 1900 to 1902, and Hobbins made no journal entries. Entries began again in the spring of 1903, but they were becoming even briefer than before. Hobbins was now into his thirties, and although it seemed he attempted to hunt at every opportunity, other life activities were probably demanding more time. The last year Hobbins kept a record was 1912.

Hunter with American water spaniel WHi Image ID 17099

Chapter 15
An Old Dog for a New Century:
The History of the American
Water Spaniel

I magine that you could design a new breed of hunting dog to meet the needs and opportunities of hunting in the twenty-first century. You'd want it to be as versatile as your hunting interests—a dog that could brave frigid Wisconsin waters and aggressively mark and retrieve waterfowl, proficiently find and flush upland birds, and be a fine rabbit or squirrel dog. Because time and space can be limited, it should be a dog easily trained and small enough to fit comfortably in canoe, skiff, or duck blind. Of course, this dog should also be a great family companion and watchdog.

Luckily, years of careful, selective breeding won't be needed to produce such an "all-around" hunter—it already exists in the form of the American water spaniel (AWS). The AWS is as "Wisconsin" as cheese, having originated more than one hundred years ago in the Fox and Wolf river valleys to meet the exacting demands of market hunters.[1] One of the few hunting breeds developed in the United States, and the only one that calls Wisconsin home, the AWS has been greatly overlooked by hunters in years past but deserves serious consideration by sports enthusiasts looking for that one dog that can do it all.

Most middle-aged or younger hunters have probably never even seen an AWS, let alone had the opportunity to hunt with one. The AWS is a medium-sized dog, on the small side compared with other retrievers, generally thirty to forty-five pounds and fifteen to eighteen inches at the shoulder. The characteristic coat can range from tightly curled to wavy, and it comes in solid brown, dark chocolate, or liver. The ears are long and lobular in shape and are thickly furred. The breed standard includes a tapered, moderately long, fully haired tail. The tail is not "rat-like" as seen in the Irish water spaniel—a rare breed sometimes confused with the AWS.

The origins of the breed date back to the period between the end of the Civil War and the turn of the century, when commercial waterfowlers along the

Fox and Wolf river valleys sought a hunting dog that could hold up under the pressures of hard work and harsh conditions. They needed a dog to plow through thick marsh and swamp vegetation to make retrieve after retrieve and to help bag muskrats and mink, hunt grouse, and get squirrels.

The exact origin of the breed may be lost to history. However, one theory explains that through nonscientific, selective breeding among market hunters who recognized that the little brown dogs with brown eyes were their best workers, a distinct breed arose (possibly with the early ancestry of Irish water spaniel and curly coated retriever).[2] This dog possessed a thick double coat to repel frigid spring and autumn waters, a coloration that blended with the browns of marsh and swamp, a long tail to serve as a rudder in swift waters, and a small size to fit easily in the market hunter's skiff, or "pole boat." This dog also possessed an innate hunting instinct coupled with a keen intelligence.

The reputation of the AWS as a rugged hunting dog that could do anything grew throughout the Upper Midwest in the late 1800s. In the early years there was no real recognition of the breed. It was often referred to as the brown water spaniel or just American brown spaniel.[3] After the market hunters faded away, the AWS was still popular with Lake States waterfowlers, but as waterfowl numbers plummeted during the dust bowl years of the 1930s, the little brown dog was in danger of slipping into oblivion as part of just another chapter of hunting history.

The breed's savior came in the form of a physician from New London, Wisconsin. Dr. F. J. Pfeifer has often been credited with saving the breed. "Doc" Pfeifer realized that the little brown hunting dogs he had known since childhood were actually a distinct breed.[4] He began breeding the dogs in 1909 and saw that litter after litter retained the same strong characteristics. Doc Pfeifer worked tirelessly to establish breed standards and gain breed recognition. His efforts led to the recognition of the AWS as a purebred by the United Kennel Club (UKC) in 1920 and by the Field Dog Stud Book in 1938.[5] Others carried on Doc's work. John Scofield of Missouri and Thomas Brogden of Rush Lake, Wisconsin, revitalized the American Water Spaniel Club (AWSC) and helped win the more prestigious American Kennel Club (AKC) recognition of the breed in 1940.[6]

Up until WWII, the AWS was a common hunting dog in Wisconsin and could be found in every small town along the Fox, Wolf, Wisconsin, and Mississippi rivers. Along with the Chesapeake Bay Retriever, another native U.S. breed, the

An Old Dog for a New Century: The History
of the American Water Spaniel

AWS was one of the few breeds used by waterfowlers in the Upper Midwest in the 1930s and '40s. After the war, the popularity of larger breeds, such as Labrador and golden retrievers, exploded, and the AWS was relegated to obscurity.

The obscurity continues to this day, keeping the AWS one of the least-known sporting dog breeds. The fact that the breed still exists and extremely high-quality pups can be located is due to a small but highly dedicated contingent of AWS breeders who continue the tradition begun by Doc Pfeifer.

John and Mary Barth began Swan Lake Kennels on their Columbia County farm in 1967. John, a native of La Crosse, recalled their decision to breed AWSs. "When I was a kid my father always had an American water spaniel," said Barth. "We hunted with them on the Mississippi, but they were great family dogs and companions as well. I always had fond memories of those dogs, and when we decided to get into dog breeding, the AWS was a natural choice."[7] The Barths developed Swan Lake into one of the leading AWS kennels in the Midwest and have shipped pups to every state except Hawaii. While John and Mary are now deceased, their daughter Ellen now runs Swan Lake Kennels.

The list of major AWS breeders is not long—most are still found in Wisconsin or adjacent states. The AWS is practically unknown outside of the United States. The dual nature of the AWS as both a competent retriever and a spaniel has left the breed "unclassified" by the AKC.[8] Without either a retriever or flushing spaniel status, the AWS cannot participate in AKC-sanctioned field trials or hunt tests and consequently lacks the exposure that other sporting breeds receive. Members of the American Water Spaniel Club, the AKC parent club of the breed, have divergent viewpoints regarding classification. Some feel the AWS cannot compete as well with typical spaniels, while others feel the breed shouldn't compete against bigger retrievers. It's a dilemma caused by the breed's versatility and won't soon be resolved. In a 1999 vote of AWSC members, the majority chose to keep the breed unclassified.

The AWSC decision may stem from the fact that most people purchase an AWS primarily because they want a dependable hunting companion, not a dog for competition.

"We sell puppies to people looking for a single dog that can do a wide range of hunting," said Mary Barth. "Many of our customers remember the hardworking little dog that their father or grandfather had."[9]

The AWS is a breed with a rich history, but it is also ready for the future.

Hunters in the twenty-first century will likely be looking for a dog that can live easily in urban or suburban environments, serve a dual role as hunting dog and trusted family companion, train easily, and, foremost, be ready to tackle anything from ducks to rabbits. Wisconsin hunters will see many changes in the years to come. Perhaps one of them will be a resurgence of Wisconsin's official state dog, the practical little American water spaniel.

Cars stuck in snow following Armistice Day Storm
Courtesy of the Minnesota Historical Society

Chapter 16
The Armistice Day Storm:
The Winds of Hell

I t began building nearly one thousand miles away, a classic "Panhandle hook" storm, a low-pressure system that would track from the southwest—the region east of the Rocky Mountains encompassing the Texas and Oklahoma Panhandles—toward the northeast, across Kansas and Iowa and into Minnesota and Wisconsin. As the system raced northward it gained strength by the hour—feeding on warm, moist air from the Gulf of Mexico to the south and a Canadian cold front in the north—intensifying into what meteorologists call a storm "bomb."[1] In its path houses and barns collapsed, chimneys toppled, trees were uprooted, and livestock froze to death in pastures and pens. When it reached the Upper Midwest the storm had become a deadly, raging fury—gale-force winds, plunging temperatures, rain and sleet, and then blinding snow. The big storm hit Wisconsin on the afternoon of November 11—Armistice Day. The year was 1940.

The storm moved with a terrifying swiftness that caught thousands of people, many outside to enjoy another day of mild November weather, completely unawares.

Minnesota and Wisconsin duck hunters were foremost among those people. The duck season ran sixty days that year, an increase of fifteen days from the 1939 season, and hunting prospects were good.[2] Mild autumn weather, however, had hampered hunter efforts. A Wisconsin newspaper reported: "Not a lack of ducks but a lack of duck weather has resulted in a poor season to date, in the opinion of F. R. Zimmerman, in charge of waterfowl studies for the conservation department." The report added, "The duck season may yet make up for lost time during the rest of this month with the prospect that there will be some real duck weather to put birds on the move."[3] The season was due to close November 29. Real duck weather was what hunters across Wisconsin were longing for—weather as it should be in Wisconsin in November: cold fronts and low, scudding clouds from the north that would bring down fat Canadian birds and stir up the local populations. But Armistice Day morning brought more unseasonably warm temperatures and quiet winds, another bluebird day. Hunters who ventured out to the marshes that morning had little need for heavy winter clothing; flannel shirts and canvas jackets sufficed. As the storm front approached from the west and the skies darkened in the afternoon, waterfowlers welcomed the change in weather, the increasing winds and cooling temperatures. Duck weather, finally.

Hunters from Wisconsin and Minnesota plying the vast backwaters, marshes, and wooded islands of the upper Mississippi River roughly between La Crosse, Wisconsin, and Red Wing, Minnesota, were the first to feel the change. As the barometric pressure plummeted to record-setting lows, the ducks responded accordingly.

"There were just a lot of birds moving," recalled Minnesota hunter Sonny Ehlers. "Ducks, there were ducks all over."[4]

But the excitement over the arrival of duck weather was short-lived. Before most hunters could react, before many could even retrieve the ducks they had just shot, the deceptively mild wind that came with the leading edge of the storm grew into a ferocious gale.

Harold Hettrick, a retired Wisconsin conservation warden, recorded his memories of the Armistice Day storm at the Smithsonian Folklife Festival on July 2, 1998. Hettrick was a high school student at the time the storm struck the Mississippi River valley:

> The weather started to deteriorate. The wind came up first. And the shooting got good. Hunters were going for their limits, which were big limits in those days. They didn't pay that much attention to the ferocity of the wind until all of a sudden it was 4 o'clock. Then it was too rough to go back. That was when the hunting season closed everyday at that time, 4 o'clock. So they were stranded out there, many in hip boots and waders and small skiffs, small boats, in marshes or on shallow islands above the water line. The wind was coming over, bringing the waves over these islands and these marshes, and as 6 o'clock came it was sub-zero. They were freezing. They were sheets of ice.[5]

The Armistice Day Storm: The Winds of Hell

Duck hunters on the Mississippi had no way of knowing that what appeared at first to be a typical autumn weather front, like so many they had hunted in the past, would in a matter of a few hours become a howling, deadly nightmare. The intensity of the storm had not been predicted, and no warnings were issued that might have kept hunters from being trapped in the field. Apparently no one from the U.S. Weather Bureau (the precursor to the National Weather Service) was watching the storm's development on the morning of November 11.[6]

By late afternoon the brunt of the storm bore down on stranded duck hunters up and down the Mississippi. Temperatures that had been in the sixties and seventies in the morning plummeted to below freezing, resulting in horrendous windchill factors when combined with winds of fifty to eighty miles per hour. Evening brought heavy snowfall, blown horizontal by the gale. The night would be long and punishing for those caught in the storm.

Many of those stranded survived only through incredible effort. Hunters forced themselves to keep active during the night—running in circles or sparring with each other—knowing that to give up would mean certain death. Hunters packed marsh grass into their hip boots and waders and under their clothing for insulation. Some built nests of marsh grass underneath overturned skiffs and hunkered down for the night. One hunter survived because his hunting dogs kept him warm.[7]

Others weren't so fortunate. With clothing soaked from rain and sleet that came as the storm approached in the afternoon, the assault of wind, bitter cold, and snow was just too much, and hunters by the score died from exposure.

The late Wisconsin outdoor writer Gordon MacQuarrie immortalized the tragedy in a newspaper account that appeared in the Winona, Minnesota, daily newspaper November 30, 1940.

MacQuarrie described the storm as perhaps the worst hunting season disaster in U.S. history.[8] He wrote about the duck hunters who died up and down the Mississippi on Armistice Day and night, caught completely unprepared for the onslaught:

The ducks came and the men died. They died underneath upturned skiffs as the blast sought them out on boggy, unprotected islands. They died trying to light fires and jumping and sparring to keep warm. They died sitting in skiffs. They died standing in river water to their hips, awaiting help.[9]

They will tell you this for years to come. They will recall how dad and brother were saved, and men who came through it alive together will look at each other with new understanding, as is the way with those who have seen death brush them close.[10]

Hunters were hit hard on the big waters of the Mississippi, but the storm didn't stop there. It continued to race eastward, gaining intensity as it swept across the state. The storm claimed another victim when it reached central Wisconsin, this time on the Big Eau Pleine reservoir, a flowage formed by the damming of the Big Eau Pleine River in southern Marathon County.

The *Wausau Daily Record-Herald* reported: "Enrollees of CCC Camp Rib Mountain and individual searching parties were patrolling the banks of the Big Eau Pleine river reservoir in the town of Green Valley today in an effort to locate Harry Zastrow, 57, town of Hamburg farmer, who was believed to have been drowned when a sudden squall struck the reservoir shortly after he started out alone on a duck hunting trip in a boat Monday noon at 12:30 o'clock."[11]

Zastrow, his son LeRoy, and a farm hand, David Smith, had set out on a duck hunt before noon on Armistice Day, probably encouraged by the change in weather and hoping that the winds would bring ducks on the wing. After meeting at a local farmer's boat landing on the shores of the flowage, LeRoy and Smith rowed their boat eastward, leaving behind the elder Zastrow, who planned to follow in a small skiff after a visit with the farmer.[12]

Zastrow "left the dock about 12:30 o'clock, just before the sudden squall, which whipped waves into heights of four and five feet on the treacherous waters, struck the spot."[13]

The storm forced LeRoy Zastrow and Smith to beach their boat and walk back several miles to the dock, their agreed-upon meeting place. The squall was so severe, LeRoy later told the Wausau reporter, that he "abandoned decoys only 20 feet from his boat."[14]

The search party finally discovered Harry Zastrow's body on an island in the reservoir. Apparently he was able to beach the boat safely but succumbed to exposure.[15]

Those duck hunters plying the larger waters of the state, such as the Mississippi and the large flowages and lakes, were most vulnerable to the storm's fury. When the winds and cold tore through the popular duck hunting marshes of the Poygan, Butte des Mortes, and Winnebago lake chain in southeast Wisconsin, havoc, suffering, and death again ensued.

"An example of the wind's force was found in reports from Fond du Lac, at the foot of Lake Winnebago, and Neenah, at the head of the lake, 40 miles north," reported the Associated Press. "At Fond du Lac one could walk 500 to 600 feet out into what ordinarily was the lake, and not get wet feet—the wind had pushed water that far from the normal shoreline."[16]

Without the benefit of advanced storm warning and communication systems, group after group of waterfowlers were caught by the storm, including dozens hunting Lake Winnebago and Lake Butte des Mortes. As Gordon MacQuarrie had done for the Mississippi River hunters, reporters in southeastern Wisconsin documented the individual life-and-death struggles that played out against a backdrop of gale-force winds, whitecapped waves, and blinding snow.

The Associated Press reported numerous harrowing tales of survival:

"Walter Haufe, 28, Neenah was rescued from the lake [Winnebago] after his skiff swamped. He stood in water up to his armpits for an hour and a half before he was noticed by the caretaker of a nearby estate."[17]

"R. J. White, Oshkosh banker, Walter Kieckhefer, Milwaukee, and William H. Brand, Milwaukee, had to spend the night on Long Point island in Lake Winnebago because the water was too rough to permit rescue. A campfire burned on the island throughout the hours of darkness."[18]

Carl Hartman, Milwaukee, was rescued from a marsh on Butte des Mortes, but suffered frostbite on feet and hands.[19] In a *Wisconsin Sportsman* article published in 1974, writer Lee Brunner documented the survival story of an individual duck hunter, Bill Davis of Oshkosh.

Davis had decided to spend Armistice Day afternoon hunting the familiar waters of Lake Butte des Mortes. Not long after he had rowed his skiff more than a mile and settled it into a marshland blind, the weather began to turn.

"As he waited he could feel the air growing colder," wrote Brunner. "Winds picking up too, he [Davis] thought. If these waves get any higher the decoys will be nosing in. He waited a short time to see if the wind would calm down, then reluctantly began picking up his decoys."[20] Other hunters in the area were doing the same. But the storm was moving faster than the hunters.

Brunner wrote that Davis barely escaped with his life that day. As he tried to get to shore, freezing rain and wind-whipped waves threatened to swamp his skiff. Only through sheer determination was Davis, clothing coated with ice, able to reach a small cabin where he hoped a friend would be present. At the cabin door he was too cold and exhausted to knock, but he managed to kick lamely with his foot. His friend was there, and his life was saved.[21]

The survivors were the fortunate ones.

"Tales of thrilling rescue and harrowing experiences were told as dozens of duck hunters were brought from lakes and marshes," reported the Associated Press. "Not all of them returned. Some drowned and some died of exposure as the 60-mile wind whipped usually placid waters to a froth. Several of those saved suffered frozen hands and feet."[22]

One of those who lost his life on Butte des Mortes was twenty-eight-year-old Oshkosh native Lawrence Boeder.

"Boeder, who with his brothers, George and Paul, went hunting on Lake Butte des Morts [sic], froze to death when raging winds brought near zero temperatures to this region during the night. The party had been trapped on an island by high waves. Paul Boeder was treated for frozen hands and feet."[23]

Neal Lendved, eighty-seven, currently a resident of Green Bay but born and raised in Kewaunee, first started duck hunting as a kid in the 1930s, mentored by his father, an avid duck hunter. He was eighteen years old when he and his father decided to venture out to a local duck lake the day after Armistice Day. On the southeast side of the state the storm's winds hadn't really peaked in the area until during the night, and they were still high in the morning. Awaking to what seemed like great duck weather on November 12, the Lendveds headed to East Alaska Lake with high expectations.

"The expedition started late that morning," recalled Lendved sixty-nine years later:

A sudden drop in temperature and gale force west wind promised good hunting. We went to East Alaska Lake, not too far from home. Using a rental boat from a livery on the west shore we headed for a small cattail island near the lake's middle. As soon as we left the shelter of the west shore it became evident that the heavy wind would not allow us to row back to the landing. There was no choice. We headed for the island.

We didn't see many ducks until the blasting wind blew us into the reeds of the island. It seemed that every duck of every kind was sheltering in those cattails. As they went out we gave them a shotgun salute. A couple of birds fell, but they were not the ones we were aiming at. The wind was so strong that the shot was blown down wind and the birds, although flying full out, only made slow progress in the wind.[24]

Because the gale would not allow Lendved and his father to row back to the boat livery, they set a course downwind and landed on the northeast shore at the farm of a friend of the elder Lendved.

"It then became my chore to walk back to the landing, make my apologies to the boat owner, retrieve our car, and pick up my dad at the farm house," remembered Neal.

At only about fifty acres in size, East Alaska Lake did not present the same challenges and dangers hunters experienced on the bigger rivers, lakes, and flowages in the midst of the storm, and the Lendveds' experience there was not enough to keep them from the field.

"Since we were slow learners," recalled Neal, "we simply went back to our home, put on drier and warmer clothes and went to a blind we had under the sheltering bluffs of Lake Michigan. The idea was that we would only shoot birds under the wind shadow of the bluff. I would retrieve them with our fourteen foot skiff."

The hunters' plan worked well at first, until one downed bird caught the wind and landed outside of the bluff's wind shadow. Attempting to retrieve the bird, Lendved's skiff also caught the wind, which threatened to take it out to the open waters of Lake Michigan. Lendved recalled:

Recovering the dead bird lost all priority. Rowing into the wind was a losing proposition, but by pulling full out and veering to the north I hoped to come across a reef that extends straight out from the shore. By heading west northwest my actual course was east northeast. After about fifteen minutes the breaking waves told me I was over the reef and an oar over the side sounded about three feet of water. So it was over the side and a long cold wading exercise. My father met me half way to shore and we pulled the boat back to shore. That ended our hunt for the day.

Neal Lendved came very close to becoming an addition to the Armistice Day storm death toll. "The fool killer was disappointed that day," Lendved joked.

On land the storm reached its greatest intensity in southeast Wisconsin. In the Milwaukee area, the temperature had dropped an incredible forty-one degrees in twelve hours. A warm fifty-seven degrees on Armistice Day morning had plummeted to sixteen degrees by 11:00 p.m. and continued to drop to thirteen degrees during the night. Winds reaching eighty miles per hour were recorded at the Milwaukee airport.

Coast guardsmen recovered the body of Edward Quick, Milwaukee, from Big Muskego Lake, located in Waukesha County southwest of Milwaukee. In an Associated Press story, two other Milwaukee hunters whose boat had frozen into the ice on Big Muskego Lake during the storm described how they witnessed Quick's plight:

"'About 30 feet from us was another man in a rowboat,' Ignatius Zielinski said. 'He didn't have any gloves on. He'd row a few strokes and then huddle up. Every once in a while he'd lift his arms, palm forward up over his shoulders toward the sun. Then he slumped over the side of the boat. Both arms dangled in the water.'"[25]

Leaving Wisconsin behind, the storm howled out across the open waters of Lake Michigan where it caused havoc with shipping lanes, grounding and sinking ships and sending hundreds scrambling for safe harbor.

Early in the storm's development, winds were from the southeast, which caused many ships on Lake Michigan to travel up and down the eastern shore of the lake, but when the brunt of the storm brought winds shifting to the southwest and west on November 11, ships became exposed and vulnerable to the full force of the gale and the crashing seas it created.

According to the Lake Huron Marine Lore Society, "While the gale was violent on Lake Huron and almost as heavy on lakes Superior and Erie, it was Lake Michigan that bore the brunt of a storm of incredible character and the longest in duration known to that body of water."[26]

An Associated Press report from Ludington, Michigan, on November 13 stated: "The grim tale of Lake Michigan's most disastrous storm in recent years unfolded slowly today as coast guardsmen, aided by subsiding seas, renewed efforts to reach stricken vessels being dashed to pieces on the rocks."[27]

The *William B. Davock* was one of two ships lost. The *Davock* sank in 210 feet of water off Pentwater, Michigan, taking with her all thirty-two men aboard and a cargo of coal.[28] The Canadian grain carrier *Anna C. Minch* was the second freighter completely destroyed during the storm, also going down near Pentwater and taking with her the entire crew of twenty-four.

The following is the text from a Michigan historical marker in Pentwater:

The most disastrous day in the history of Lake Michigan shipping was Armistice (now Veterans') Day, November 11, 1940. With seventy-five-mile-per-hour winds and twenty-foot waves, a raging storm destroyed three ships and claimed the lives of fifty-nine seamen. Two freighters sank with all hands lost, and a third, the *Novadoc*, ran aground with the loss of two crew members. Bodies washed ashore throughout the day. As night fell, a heavy snow storm arrived. Rescue efforts by the Coast Guard and local citizens continued for three days after the storm. Three Pentwater fishermen were later recognized by the local community and the Canadian government for their bravery in rescuing seventeen sailors from the *Novadoc*.[29]

As the Armistice Day storm began to abate on November 13, Wisconsin residents started to tally the losses in lives and property from what had been the most horrendous storm most had ever experienced. For days afterward, family, friends, and local officials combed Wisconsin shorelines and marshes for the missing.

"Searching parties pushed forward today on the grim task of hunting more victims as Wisconsin took stock of her losses in the death-dealing gale of Monday and Tuesday," reported the Associated Press on November 13.[30]

When the counting was completed, a total of 154 lives lost were attributed to the Armistice Day storm.[31] Minnesota suffered the heaviest toll with forty-nine dead; about half of those were duck hunters.[32] Thirteen Wisconsin deaths were attributed to the storm, many of those duck hunters as well. Another fifty-nine deaths were related to the shipping disasters on Lake Michigan.[33]

For years afterward, old duck hunters told stories of the Armistice Day storm—tales of courage, survival, and death.

Vern Frechette (left) and Leonard Larson with a catch of trout Courtesy of Mike Frechette

Chapter 17
One Day in March 1933

Every one of us has a story—a story of that one incident, that most exciting event in our lives. It is the story we tell and retell through the years and somehow becomes its own entity. It becomes "Dad's story" or "Uncle Joe's story," guaranteed to be heard at gatherings of old friends, or family reunions, or just over any late-night cup of coffee.

The event that was to become Vern Frechette's story, a story he has told countless times during the past seventy years, had its subtle birth on what looked to be a pretty fair morning for fishing in early March 1933.

Frechette is ninety-three years old now and lives in an apartment in Washburn, the small town directly across Chequamegon Bay from Ashland. He can't get around as he used to, or as he'd like to. His knees bother him, and he can't drive anymore. The years have robbed him of much of his hearing. He misses the outdoors—the hunting and the fishing that took him to every quiet corner of the Bayfield Peninsula. Born and raised on Chequamegon Bay, he knew it better than most. He also knew the offshore waters and the sometimes-calm, sometimes-angry waters between the Apostles—Long Island, Madeline, Michigan—waters fished heavily by Frechette and other locals and today often plied by tourists in big boats.

The morning of March 9 looked like a pretty good morning to get out on the ice, and Vern, his brother George, and friend Oscar Holman navigated a Model T to the ice between the northeast end of Madeline Island and Michigan Island. About ten other men from Washburn and a handful from Ashland were also on the ice that day.

The men were after big lake trout, the heavy fish that could feed a family or be sold over at Cornucopia sometimes for twenty-three cents a pound. Lake trout run deep, and fishing for them in the 1930s meant using a big bobbing hook and heavy "tarred" line.

"What we did was take shoemaker's twine and twist two or three strands together, and then we stretched it out and tarred it," Frechette told me. "It held up pretty good, but you had to check on it pretty often."[1]

Store-bought hooks were rare back then. The hooks were sometimes fashioned from the tines of a pitchfork. "Those hooks didn't have eyelets on them like today," Frechette said. "We attached the line to the hook by wrapping the end with thread and then sealing it with nail polish." He continued, "We tied on a heavy lead sinker shaped like a cone and used cut bait—cut up herring and such—for bait."

Trout fishing on Lake Superior ice in early March was serious business. But the threat of a storm coming up from the southwest was big business, too, and when the wind began to blow across the ice the Frechette brothers knew just what to do—pack up and get to land as fast as possible.

As they drove the Model T toward Long Island, the storm intensified surprisingly, with temperatures plunging and a driving snow developing.

"Driving back we could suddenly see an open stretch of water running south from Madeline Island, and it was steadily growing wider," said Frechette.

The Frechette brothers and the twenty-seven other fisherman out on the ice that day had become trapped on an ice floe that was being blown out to the open lake by the intensifying storm. Their lives were in jeopardy, and everyone knew it.

"We didn't have time to be scared," said Frechette. "We just had to get off the ice somehow."

Stopped at the edge of the floe and looking toward the island that now seemed so far away, the three men saw a vision through the storm. A man was rowing a fourteen-foot-long flat-bottomed boat through the waves.

The man was Bancroft Bufe, a fisherman from Grand Marais, Michigan, and he was rowing for all he was worth. Bufe had just rescued Oscar Anderson of Ashland and Lester Lindblad of Washburn, but when he saw the Frechette brothers and Oscar Holman, he turned course and returned to the floe to add three more souls to the small boat.[2]

On the shore of Madeline Island people were watching the rescue unfold. "The waves were getting higher, and we'd go up and down on them. Each time we dropped from sight, the people on shore thought we had gone down," said Frechette.

The wind was fierce, and the men's clothes were freezing to their skin. Chunks of ice were punching holes in the small boat, and while Bufe rowed, the others bailed out water with a wooden box. Oscar Holman tried to relieve Bufe, but "he almost lost it," and Bufe, experienced with his boat, took back control and continued the slow movement toward shore.

"We had reached the edge of the ice floe at about 9:00 or 10:00 a.m.," said Frechette. "It must have been about noon when we reached the beach at Long Island."

With frozen clothes the six men walked along the beach toward Madeline Island and finally reached the shack of Billy Bryan. "My clothes were frozen so stiff that I had to stand by the stove for an hour before I could bend my arms," said Frechette.

Similar feats of rescue and escape were repeated across the ice floe. Ole Sandstrom and George LaRock of Madeline Island saved themselves by walking in an easterly direction all day on the ice floe until they could get to shore near Saxon Harbor.[3] Amazingly, all twenty-nine people who had been caught on the ice floe that day were rescued or escaped unharmed, although several cars, abandoned by their owners, forever became property of Lake Superior.

The *Ashland Daily Press* reported:

Tales of heroism and miraculous rescue in rough water, and reports of men still adrift on the ice floes east of Long Island including one man who was last seen kneeling in prayer as he was lost from sight by eight others who had been rescued, were collected throughout the night last night by the *Daily Press* as the aftermath of the breaking off of a huge ice cake which threatened the lives of many residents of the Chequamegon region.[4]

All the survivors became a part of an incredible story that for years was the staple of local barbershops and taverns around Chequamegon Bay. Today, Vern Frechette is the sole keeper of the story, the last one who can say he was there.

Not many people ask about that day in March 1933 anymore, but Vern's memories of the day are as sharp as ever. "Oh, we took some awful chances out there," he told me, as he described how he and the other fishermen would lay planks across the cracks in the ice as bridges to get the vehicles across.

With a grin on his face and shining eyes, he summed up that day on the ice simply. "Oh, it throws a scare into you," he said.

Dwight Eisenhower (second from left) and his brothers pose with catch
WHi Image ID 2095

Chapter 18
Ike's First Vacation
to the Wisconsin Northwoods

The fighting in Europe had been over for little more than a year by the summer of 1946, but for U.S. Army chief of staff General Dwight D. Eisenhower the work was far from over. Ike, the American hero who had served as supreme commander of Allied forces in the European theater of WWII and who had directed the monumental assault against the Nazis on the northern French coast at Normandy, now found himself in Washington, DC, immersed in peacetime politics. The army was being demobilized, the Soviet Union was emerging as a postwar threat, and America was divided over its future as a nuclear power.

The postwar turmoil was enough to make the general, who was known for working twenty-hour days during the war, think about taking a vacation. A chance meeting between Eisenhower and Wisconsin governor Walter Goodland's secretary, Frank Graas, earlier in the year had resulted in an invitation for Ike to rest, relax, and do a little fishing in northern Wisconsin.[1] The general accepted the offer, and plans were quietly laid for a real northwoods fishing trip to the heart of the lakes country near Minocqua.

General Eisenhower arrived in Minocqua in the late morning of Monday, July 15, aboard a Milwaukee Road passenger train. His four brothers, Edgar, Milton, Arthur, and Earl, accompanied him—the first time the five Eisenhower boys had vacationed together in twenty years.

The vacation plans had been kept as secret as an army invasion plan by Ike's staff, as the general truly desired some quality relaxation time. Although there wasn't advance fanfare, word of the general's vacation did manage to reach the Island City just prior to his arrival. By Sunday night the word had spread like wildfire around town, which put city officials in a delicate position. The official request from the army was that no fancy, formal welcome be given—but this was

Eisenhower, the man who had accepted unconditional surrender from the Nazis only months before. It was decided that, at the very least, a display of American flags up and down Oneida Avenue would be appropriate.[2]

A large crowd of Minocqua residents and summer tourists were on hand when the 10:50 a.m. train pulled into the Milwaukee Road depot, but their hopes of seeing much of Ike were short-lived. The general and his party wasted little time as they climbed into the waiting cars and were quickly taken out of town. Lawrence Bradley, Minocqua's chief of police at the time, was left to manage the large, milling crowd. Town of Minocqua chairman John J. O'Leary helped untangle the mess.[3]

Governor Goodland, known across the state as "the Tough Codger" for his brassy style, telegraphed a welcome to the Eisenhowers:

> I am delighted and pleased that you have been able to visit Wisconsin as planned and discussed with my secretary in Oklahoma City. I am quite aware of your desire for privacy and rest. Therefore, I send this written welcome instead of a personal visit. I trust that our preparations for your vacation will be satisfactory to you and your brothers.
>
> Please be assured that the governor's office, the motor vehicle department and the conservation department are completely at your service. Every person in Wisconsin joins with me in wishing you complete privacy, rest, recreation and good fishing in our vacationland.[4]

Though the eighty-three-year-old governor honored the general's request for a quiet arrival, he intended to make certain Eisenhower and his party had a vacation to remember.

State police were assigned to guard the entourage, and two fishing guides were appointed from the Conservation Department, Conservation Warden Harley T. McKeague of Rhinelander and State Forester William Waggoner of Trout Lake, known to be two of the most experienced guides in the department.[5]

The field headquarters for the Eisenhower vacation was Moody's Big Woods Lodge, about eight miles west of Boulder Junction. Eisenhower's northwoods host at the lodge was LeRoy Eagin, Milton Eisenhower's father-in-law.[6]

Amazingly, the Eisenhower party was able to travel the backroads of northern Wisconsin and pursue musky on the lakes of Vilas County with relatively little press coverage. What was reported was low key and always hugely positive.

"General Dwight D. Eisenhower, always a leader, set the pace for his brothers yesterday as the five men each bagged a legal size muskie on Pine Lake, in Vilas County, in a remarkable exhibition of fishing ability," reported *The Rhinelander Daily News* on July 18.

"'Ike' caught his fish exactly one hour after the party started out, and Warden Harley T. McKeague of Rhinelander gaffed the muskie after the Army chief of staff had played it for 16 minutes. 'Ike' himself walloped the fish with a stick to administer the coup de grace."[7]

The day continued to produce northwoods fishing excitement for the Eisenhowers, with plenty of strikes that enabled each brother to bag his own musky. Milton Eisenhower landed a northern pike that was reported to be "plenty big."

"Warden McKeague reported that the phenomenal luck of the Eisenhower brothers didn't apply only to fishing. He said the day was perfect for muskie fishing—a light wind, an overcast sky and no mosquitoes. He said he had never seen muskies strike so hard and so fast in one day's fishing," reported the press.[8]

As the fishing adventures drew to a close, the general made a little more time for the public and the media.

Prior to his departure on July 21, Ike, dressed in his army uniform, visited the state YMCA camp at Boulder Junction, the only planned public appearance of the entire vacation. The press snapped photos as 168 young boys clamored around the chief of staff, demanding autographs.[9]

Eisenhower mentioned the YMCA camp visit to Kris Gilbertson of *The Rhinelander Daily News* during a brief interview at the Minocqua depot: "He (Eisenhower) apparently had enjoyed the experience for he grinned with delight while telling about the way in which the boys had issued orders to him."

General Eisenhower had one last meeting planned before he headed south. He had arranged for a personal meeting with a high school-age Wisconsin girl named Jacqueline "Jackie" Halverson, Manitowoc, who had written a letter to him a year before.

Jackie Halverson's uncle, a sergeant with the army in Germany at the time, bet his niece, who had been stricken with infantile paralysis, a dollar that if she wrote to the supreme commander she would receive a reply. Thinking that a person as important and busy as Eisenhower would never have time to reply to a schoolgirl's letter, she was surprised and excited when she received a note from the general: "I appreciate your note and good wishes," he wrote. "It was most kind of you to write."[10]

Halverson's letter must have made a big impression on Ike, and a personal meeting with Jackie factored into his Wisconsin vacation plans.

"A letter written to Gen. Dwight D. Eisenhower on a bet more than a year ago paid off today for Jacqueline Halverson, 18, in the form of an invitation to spend a day with the Army's chief of staff at his Minocqua vacation headquarters," reported the Associated Press.[11]

Time constraints allowed for only a quick meeting between General Eisenhower and Halverson at the train depot prior to Ike's departure, but that was plenty for the girl.

Gilbertson spoke with her and reported on the event in the *Rhinelander Daily News*:

> I talked to "Jackie" before the general arrived and she was so nervous she found it difficult to sit still. She wanted to know what to talk about when she did meet the Army boss.
>
> The general and his brothers arrived in two cars driven by state traffic officers, and as soon as "Ike" got out of the car in which he was riding he went over to greet Miss Halverson. He willingly posed with "Jackie" for a picture taken by the girl's mother, who said afterwards she hoped she remembered to snap the shutter properly.[12]

At the Milwaukee Road depot in Minocqua, General Eisenhower willingly answered questions from the press about his weeklong fishing trip to the northwoods.

"You can tell people that the five Eisenhower brothers are agreed that they could not have chosen a more pleasant vacation location," he stated. "Everything has been wonderful. The fishing was excellent—I got two muskies you know—and the weather conditions were very, very pleasant."[13]

The general and his group had experienced the perfect northwoods fishing trip, and he was sincerely impressed. The vacation of 1946 was destined to be only the first of many trips Eisenhower made to the lakeland area.

According to *Lakeland Times* writer Joyce Laabs, it was on this first outing that Eisenhower met the wealthy New York City art dealer and Republican Party supporter (and uncle to actress Elizabeth Taylor) Howard Young. Young owned a summer lodge in the Minocqua area.[14]

Young, an ardent fisherman himself, had managed to get past the state police guarding Moody's resort and meet the general by brandishing a stringer of fat bass.[15] Young also was one of the founders of the Minocqua Country Club, and he invited Ike to golf there. With both men possessing a love for fishing and golf, they quickly became close friends.

On all subsequent vacations to the Minocqua area, Dwight and Mamie Eisenhower would be guests of Howard Young and would stay at his estate on Lake Minocqua. The Eisenhowers would visit again in 1948, 1965, and 1967.[16]

President Coolidge on the Bois Brule WHi Image ID 2093

Chapter 19
The Summer White House
on the Brule

C alvin Coolidge served as president of the United States from 1923 to 1929. Coolidge, vice president in Warren G. Harding's administration, initially gained the presidency following Harding's sudden death by stroke in August of 1923. The "Roaring Twenties" were a time of great prosperity as well as great social change in America. A growing fear of communism, prohibition and the organized crime wave it spawned, and the debate over the teaching of evolution in schools signified that the nation was undergoing inexorable change. The president known as "silent Cal" for his minimalist use of words, however, remained as quiet and steady as ever. His daily routine included going to bed early, getting up early, taking a two- or three-hour nap in the afternoon, and perhaps relaxing in a rocking chair on the front porch of the White House with a fine Havana cigar.

His conservative philosophy held that government, including the office of the president, should interfere as little as possible in the lives of its citizens. This policy won him the distinction of also being known as the "passive president." So it was not out of character for Coolidge to pack up his belongings and temporarily move the "White House," and thus the center of American politics, to a fishing lodge on the relatively remote Bois Brule River, a few miles south of the small northern Wisconsin town called Brule in Douglas County, for the summer of 1928.

The precedent for a summer White House had already been set by Coolidge the year before when he and his wife, Grace, spent an entire month in the Black Hills of South Dakota, staying at the state game lodge there. It was from the Black Hills that he issued the famous statement, "I do not choose to run for President in 1928."[1] Without the tedium of a campaign to worry about, Coolidge made plans to spend nearly the entire summer on the banks of the Bois Brule River—fishing, relaxing, and sometimes tending to the affairs of the United States.

In the spring of 1928 an announcement was made that Coolidge would be spending the summer at the estate of the late Henry Clay Pierce.[2] Pierce, a wealthy financier and oilman from St. Louis, had begun to acquire properties along the upper Brule in the late 1800s, including a lodge building on Cedar Island.[3] Through the years, Pierce endeavored to create a vast wilderness preserve for himself, buying up land until he owned 106 forties.[4] He also enlarged the original Cedar Island lodge and added a dining hall, servants' quarters, and a superintendent's house.[5] The entire estate was fenced and posted and remained a curious mystery to most residents of Brule and Douglas County.

Although Henry Clay Pierce died in June 1927, the five heirs of his estate offered Cedar Island as a summer headquarters to President Coolidge at the urging of Wisconsin senator Irvine L. Lenroot (Republican from Superior), who owned a summer cottage on the Brule.[6] It is interesting that Lenroot, a progressive Republican, had lost the vice presidential nomination to Coolidge at the 1920 Republican National Convention in Chicago. Had Lenroot won the nomination, he, rather than Coolidge, would likely have become the thirtieth president of the United States. Coolidge accepted the Pierces' offer willingly, and he arrived at Brule on June 13, 1928. The president was accompanied by no fewer than sixty soldiers, fourteen house servants, ten secret service agents, and about seventy-five reporters.[7]

The arrival of the president of the United States and his entourage was the most exciting event to ever hit rural northwest Wisconsin. For weeks prior to Coolidge's arrival, local and state officials, businessmen, and the general citizenry scrambled to prepare for the president.

The Associated Press reported: "'Well,' said the citizens of Brule, all 200 of them, 'We must dress the place up a bit.' They cast a reflective eye down the five streets and over the three town pumps.

"But that was two full days after the news had plumped down in their midst that President and Mrs. Calvin Coolidge had decided to spend their vacation on the Henry Clay Pierce estate on Brule river. It took Brule that long to get its breath."[8]

The "dressing up" included "wooden arches of native rough timber" erected over the main road through town for which Brule citizens themselves had to "chip in" because Brule had no local government.[9] It was well known that silent Cal and his wife were staunch churchgoers, and it was correctly surmised that they would be attending weekly services in Brule. The Congregational Church there received a fresh coat of paint as well as a new roof.[10]

Looking to take advantage of the surge of activity, opportunists poured into town. "The 200 residents of this village of twenty-six cabins and other structures are riding on the greatest wave of prosperity in the community's history," reported the Associated Press on June 3. "Since Brule was selected as the place where the President would spend his vacation, rents have skyrocketed 700 per cent. Trading for business sites today was feverish."[11]

Outside of town, preparations were made as well, and in a big way. While Coolidge planned to spend most of his time at Cedar Island, he was still president of the United States and had the affairs of the country to manage. As he had the previous summer in South Dakota, Coolidge and his staff chose a high school to serve as the base for his executive office. Superior Central High School (torn down in 2003), about thirty miles by road from Cedar Island, became a hub of activity as the location where Coolidge would conduct business, receive official guests, and communicate with Washington. The school library became Coolidge's personal office. The high school was transformed into a communications nerve center, albeit 1920s style.

Even small settlements in the region saw changes due to the president's visit. According to Albert M. Marshall in his 1954 book *Brule Country*, "Governor Zimmerman of Wisconsin ordered the roads between Winneboujou, Lake Nebagamon, and Superior given preferential treatment. As a result all the unsurfaced portions were asphalted. The section between Poplar and Brule which swung south to touch the village of Lake Nebagamon and the Winneboujou community had formerly borne an undistinguished alphabetical lettering designation. Now it was proudly called the 'President Coolidge Memorial Highway.'"[12]

All the hustle and bustle regarding Coolidge's visit was big news, and quiet little places such as Brule and Lake Nebagamon suddenly were thrust into the national spotlight. Locally, however, the most talked about issue focused more on Coolidge and his fishing intentions on the Bois Brule than it did on national politics. As it still is today, fishing was serious business on Wisconsin's most famous of trout waters. Speculation about silent Cal ran through Douglas County like wildfire.

"Recollections of reports from the Black Hills of South Dakota last summer, that Mr. Coolidge went for trout with worms as bait, had aroused serious sporting misapprehensions in all devout anglers here," reported the press.[13] The press reminded folks that the late Henry Clay Pierce reportedly "never allowed anyone ever to set foot on the estate who indulged in anything but fly fishing."[14]

Calvin Coolidge was not known for his outdoor abilities. The only son of a storekeeper from Vermont, his recreational interests included golf and horseback riding. He was known for his business skill, his impeccable honesty, and his devotion to fine cigars but not for his sporting prowess. He did, however, develop a latent interest in fishing.

While vacationing at White Pines Camp on Osgood Lake, the summer estate of wealthy Kansas City publisher Irwin R. Kirkwood, in New York's Adirondack State Park in 1926, Coolidge tried his hand at fishing with secret service chief Colonel Edmund W. Starling. "In the afternoons he tried fishing with Colonel Starling and developed a zest for the sport," wrote Ishbel Ross in *Grace Coolidge and Her Era: The Story of a President's Wife*.[15]

Coolidge became a trout fishing aficionado of sorts the next year when he and Grace spent part of the summer in the Black Hills. According to Ross, although the region abounded with good trout water, Coolidge was very successful at catching trout due in no small part to Colonel Starling's "arrangements for the streams to be stocked at certain points with game trout, held in check by steel-mesh nets sunk across the stream, with logs concealing them."[16] After his experience in the Black Hills, Coolidge intended to take full advantage of the incredible fishing opportunities the Brule offered.

There is a certain culture, a time-honored trout fishing culture steeped in tradition, that permeates the Bois Brule River unlike any other fishing culture found in Wisconsin. The guides who work the canoes and find the fish for the visiting sports and wealthy lodge owners—the ones who know every riffle, every rock on the Brule—have always been central to that culture.

The most obvious choice for a guide for President Coolidge was the most veteran and most experienced guide on the river at the time, seventy-seven-year-old French-Indian Antoine Dennis. Dennis, a native of Madeline Island, had spent a lifetime in the woods around the Brule River and Lake Superior. The son of a French fur trader, he had helped early explorers navigate the region, worked as a river driver, and packed the mail by foot as well as by dogsled from Superior to Bayfield.[17] He had been guiding fishermen on the Brule for nearly forty years and had served as a guide for Herbert Hoover several years prior to Coolidge's visit to the Brule. Dennis, however, declined an offer to guide for the president, citing failing eyesight and declining strength.[18]

"It was to the Indian's home, this forest, that President Coolidge came for his vacation, too late in Dennis' life, however, and the old guide turned to a younger man to take the responsibility," reported the Associated Press.[19]

The younger man recommended as a replacement by Dennis was his son-in-law John LaRock, also of French-Indian descent and also a highly respected, veteran Brule River guide. Coolidge accepted the recommendation and hired LaRock to be his primary guide for the summer.

"John LaRock, the Indian guide who filled most of the President's guiding assignment became overnight the undisputed dean of the rivermen," wrote Marshall. "His views on the President and on his ability with rod and fly were eagerly sought after."[20]

LaRock—confident, stalwart, photogenic, and like Coolidge not one to waste words—was the perfect choice. Photos of the man often referred to simply as "Coolidge's guide" frequented local and state newspapers, and the press closely followed his activities. When LaRock sprained his back while cranking an automobile, the newspapers ran the headline: "Guide Injured, President Tries Trap Shooting."[21]

In her 1978 reminiscences of time spent on the Brule River as a child and adult, Rebekah Knight Cochran, who knew LaRock and his family, wrote: "John was a famous and outstanding man. Part French and Chippewa. Like Jack Condekon, he never drank and was always immaculate in dress and manners. Many articles have been written about him. One of Nature's noblemen."[22]

LaRock was paid two dollars per day to guide the president, and the two spent a considerable amount of time together on the dark waters of the Brule, although probably most of it in peaceful silence.[23] Coolidge took easily to the almost daily routine of climbing into his favorite Cedar Island canoe, *Beaver Dick*, with LaRock in the stern and Coolidge's white collie Rob Roy ever present in the center, to ply the Brule's secret trout holes.

Though Coolidge was recognized as a fly-fishing novice, the press corps was always complimentary. Marshall wrote: "Newsmen who covered the Presidential doings contrived to give the impression that the chief executive instead of endangering the reputation of the Brule as a good trout stream was actually turning in a fine performance."[24]

From the very first reports of Coolidge's fishing activity, the ever-important worm issue was close at hand. Eager to get some fishing in, Coolidge broke out his fishing pole within hours of his and Grace's arrival at Cedar Island. "Apparently impatient to essay the first fishing of his vacation, the president took out his fishing pole not long after his arrival and tried his luck both in the Brule and at Lake Nebagamon where he was taken in the afternoon," reported the press.[25] It also was reported that he had asked for worms.

Another report of Coolidge's first few fishing excursions noted: "Whether he had any luck or even whether he used a lowly worm instead of the fancy flies Brule trout are accustomed to was not divulged."[26]

Several days after the Coolidges' arrival at Cedar Island, reports began to surface seemingly designed to put the worm issue to bed. Perhaps after catching wind of the importance that Coolidge not be perceived as a worm man, White House staff or the press itself rescued Coolidge's reputation as a bait fisherman with firm reports that the president was not using worms to catch trout on the Brule.

"Brule tradition has been upheld by President Coolidge who has foresworn his customary fish bait by disdaining worms and using flies during his angling expeditions from the summer White House," reported the Duluth press on June 22.[27]

Another report stated: "The fishing community of Douglas County—and this comprises about three-fourths of the men, women and children within its borders—heave a great sigh of relief today to discover that President Coolidge has maintained inviolate the immemorial tradition of the Brule River of never having any of its trout caught except by dry fly fishing."[28]

However, one press report, claiming to have settled the issue, muddied the waters by contradicting the other reports: "John LaRock, President Coolidge's Indian guide, says that the chief executive is a good fisherman and 'can catch fish too.' He also declared yesterday that the president uses both worms and dry flies, settling definitely the troubling question as to what bait the president uses."[29]

Coolidge clearly reveled in fishing the Brule, and he did so as often as possible. Concern was raised that he was ignoring his duties, infrequently venturing to his office in Superior. He also seemed to be paying little attention to the world of politics as if retiring from the political scene.

"Paddling a canoe up the Brule river is more interesting to President Coolidge than the Democratic national convention which opened at Houston today," reported the *Duluth Herald* after Coolidge mostly ignored the event. "Attention to business routine and recreation are again on the schedule today, with the president more anxious to master the paddling of a canoe against the Brule rapids than in learning what is going on at the Democratic convention. John LaRock, the chief executive's Indian guide, has been teaching him how to keep the craft on its course and he is confident that his pupil will master the art before very long."[30]

As the summer on the Brule came to a close in early September, Coolidge squeezed in one last Brule River outing.

The press reported, "A last fishing excursion was organized by President Coolidge early today despite the nearness of his departure. John LaRock, his faithful Chippewa Indian guide, who since June has been taking the chief executive on the swift waters of the Brule, was on hand for a last paddle on the stream."[31]

The president departed northern Wisconsin on September 10 after a brief farewell address in Superior:

The time has come to say goodbye. We came here some weeks ago when summer was just beginning and now that the first touch of the north wind is changing the foliage to crimson and gold we are returning to Washington. We have had a wonderful summer, in large part because of the wonderful hospitality that has been extended to us by all the people of this region. Our house at Cedar Island and the surroundings there have been exceedingly pleasant. It has been an inspiration to attend the Sunday services of the blind preacher at the little church at Brule, who is compensated by the sharpness of his spiritual sight for the lack of physical sight.[32]

The newspapers made special note of the following remarks:

I think this is going to be a coming region for those who are seeking recreation. The fishing around here, I can testify, is fine. The climate is wonderful. It has been a great benefit to Mrs. Coolidge and myself, and we are returning to Washington refreshed and invigorated.

There is little doubt that Coolidge was deeply touched by the magic of the Bois Brule River during the summer of 1928, the summer when he learned to fly-fish for trout and paddle a birch bark canoe. Coolidge made no mention of John LaRock in his farewell speech, but the speech didn't contain many specifics anyway, true to Coolidge's spare use of words. According to Rebekah Knight Cochran: "When the Pres. left by private train from Winneboujou, a baggage car was filled with guns and fishing rods he had received as Pres. When his guide, John LaRock, returned to our place that day, we asked him what present he had received from the Pres. as a gift. Nothing but an autographed picture. It was on a shelf in my pantry until the next summer, when I threw it away."[33]

Although Coolidge stated he would like to return to Cedar Island, it never was to be. After his term expired Coolidge withdrew from public life. Distressed by the Great Depression, he died in January 1933, a little more than four years after the summer of the White House on the Brule.

Perhaps some foggy recollections of those carefree days spent on the Brule were passing through Coolidge's mind when, on his deathbed, he uttered his last words: "I feel I no longer fit with these times."

Passengers on the *Pelican* Courtesy of the author

Chapter 20
Murder at Pelican Lake

Hunters and trappers spend a great deal of time alone in the woods, and outdoor activities in remote areas have their share of inherent dangers. In the early 1930s, the Wisconsin northwoods held extra dangers, with large tracts of remote, logged-over country, limited communications, and few heavily traveled roads along with occasional gangsters, moonshiners, and poachers.

Edward Keeler didn't worry about dangers in the woods. The son of the first white settlers in the township of Enterprise, Oneida County, Keeler had grown up in wild, sparsely settled places. An accomplished fur trapper, hunter, and fishing guide, he was a rugged man who was at home in the woods. He had no reason to believe that another routine trip to his trapping shack in early December 1931 would be his last.

Born in 1871 in Sand Lake, Michigan, Keeler accompanied his family to the Green Bay area in 1878 and then to Enterprise in 1888 after his father inquired in Antigo about good land to homestead. Edward was seventeen years old when his family made its way to Enterprise.[1] The young Keeler developed a deep and passionate love for the northern Wisconsin outdoors at a time when many saw the northwoods only as a resource to be exploited. At the time of the Keeler family's move to Enterprise many Native Americans lived in the area, and Edward learned much about hunting, trapping, and tracking from them. He eventually became a well-known woodsman in the area as well as a highly respected citizen.

Edward's father, George Keeler, owned and operated a resort on Pelican Lake, near Enterprise, and Edward served as a fishing guide on the lake for many years.[2] The resourceful Keeler owned and operated a forty-person motorized boat on Pelican Lake during the tourist season. With his boat, the *Pelican*, Keeler picked up tourists from the railroad depot in the little village of Pelican, situated on the eastern shore of Pelican Lake, and transported them to the many resorts on the large lake and gave boat tours as well. He also delivered mail, fresh dairy products, bakery goods, and produce to the resorts. Keeler's beautifully designed and constructed boat, which sported an inboard motor, was the pride of Pelican Lake.

During the winter, Keeler earned money by running a furbearer trapline. He eventually built a small trapping shack back in the woods about three miles north of his home. In his later years he retired from the passenger boat service and began spending more time in pursuit of hunting, fishing, and trapping ventures. It was typical for Keeler to pack a few days' worth of supplies and head out to the shack to run his trapline, hunt, or just explore the woods and swamps.

On Thursday, December 3, 1931, Keeler, sixty years old at the time, left home for a two-day trip to the cabin. He told his family he would be home by Saturday. When Keeler failed to return as expected, family members became concerned—it wasn't like him to change plans without letting someone know.[3] Keeler's son, Edwin, went to the cabin looking for his father and discovered that Edward had dropped off the supplies, but the water and food were frozen. It looked as though no one had been in the cabin for a day or two. A search of the area by Edwin on Saturday, hampered by fresh snow that had covered any tracks, yielded no clues to the whereabouts of his father.[4]

Another unsuccessful search for Keeler was conducted that Sunday. The next day, county officials organized a search posse of more than fifty men led by Oneida County sheriff Hans Rodd. The posse scoured the woods in the vicinity of the shack. During the search, the body of Edward Keeler was found by his brother, Clifton Keeler, facedown in the snow in a pool of frozen blood.[5]

Sheriff Rodd pieced together what had happened by examining the clues at the scene. The sheriff's conclusion about Keeler's last minutes was gruesome. Apparently, Keeler had been walking along with his pack on his back, probably believing he was quite alone in the December woods. From about fifty yards away, an unknown person fired a .30–30 rifle at Keeler, a single shot striking him in the abdomen.[6]

The shooter would have been hidden by brush, and according to reports the single bullet passed through a two-inch-diameter tamarack tree before hitting Keeler. There was no evidence that the shooter did anything more than continue on his way, even though Keeler did not die instantly and probably was able to cry out, according to the sheriff.[7]

The mortally wounded man was able to stumble to a nearby stump, where he sat down to rest. He never got up. Bleeding from the wound, he eventually slumped forward into the snow and bled to death. The deputy county coroner from Rhinelander estimated that Keeler had been dead for at least two days prior to the discovery of the body. Because snow covered his body, officials knew he had been shot sometime before Saturday evening.[8]

The death of Edward Keeler presented a real mystery for officials. Two theories were offered as possible explanations for the shooting. The official theory was that Keeler was mistaken for a deer by a game violator who shot at movement or sound through the brush and then in a cowardly manner skipped out when realizing a man was shot.

"Although Sheriff Hans Rodd and Deputy Coroner Rudolph Carlson were still continuing their investigation this afternoon," reported the *Rhinelander Daily News* on December 7, 1931, "it is believed Oneida county officers probing the death of Edward Keeler, Enterprise farmer, will advance the theory that he was shot and killed by a game violator who mistook him for a deer."[9]

The second, less prominent theory was that Keeler was murdered in cold blood by someone bearing a grudge against the man.

Supporting the more plausible "accidental shooting by a violator" theory, both the sheriff and deputy coroner were convinced that the shooter knew he had injured a man with the reckless shot but chose to flee the scene without offering any assistance to the dying Keeler. This idea simply appalled officials and local residents.

County officials investigated the shooting further but never could discover the identity of the person who had fired the fatal shot. No one was ever arrested or charged with the crime. The town of Enterprise was rife with theories and rumors about the shooting at the time, with some holding firmly to the belief that Keeler was murdered. John Mistely, an early resident of Enterprise, now in his nineties, knew Edward Keeler well and was a member of the search party back in '31.

"Edward's death remains a mystery to this day," Mistely said. "I guess no one will ever know what really happened."[10]

Eventually most Keeler family members moved away from Enterprise and Pelican Lake, and today few people related to Edward Keeler remain. But on the west side of Pelican Lake there is a small public boat landing where a sign welcomes recreationists to the very place where Edward Keeler had regularly launched the *Pelican* well more than half a century ago. An interpretative sign at the landing says a few words about Edward, his father, and the history of the landing. Hundreds of modern-day sports enthusiasts today launch their own vessels at Keeler's landing, but few are aware of the mystery surrounding the brutal death of Edward Keeler.

Carl Schels on an expedition Courtesy of Ken Schels

Chapter 21
Trapping in the Blood:
The Carl Schels Story

I t started in late October 1929. Investors, losing confidence in the faltering U.S. economy, began unloading stocks. Panic developed and swept through Wall Street like a Kansas twister, and by mid-November the stock market had crashed, signaling the beginning of the Great Depression. In those few days fortunes were wiped out, and the prosperity of the 1920s screeched to a halt. In the months that followed hundreds of factories and mills closed their doors, and millions of American men found they were unemployed. One of those men was Carl Schels.

When the young, unmarried Schels lost his job working for Chicago Western Electric in 1930, his prospects for the future didn't look good. A Bavarian immigrant with a strong European accent and only a high school education, he had few choices. He could stand in long lines with the hundreds of other unemployed men hoping to find some menial work, or perhaps he could take to selling apples or shining shoes as some men were forced to do. He could depend on the charity of others and line up at the soup kitchens, or he could depend on the generosity of relatives. Schels chose none of those. Instead, he packed all his belongings in a Model T he had purchased for twenty dollars and drove to the Wisconsin northwoods.

"The depression was in evidence all about me and therefore, with the enthusiasm of youth, I started on my way up to the northwoods thinking that here would be my opportunity to make a fortune, little realizing that a city boy does not always find it easy to survive in the rigorous life of a woodsman," wrote the late Schels in his autobiographical book, *A Trapper's Legacy: The Tales of a Twentieth Century Trapper*.[1]

His dream was to make a living from the land somewhere in the cutover of northern Wisconsin, where thousands of acres stripped of big timber a generation before lay abandoned to wildfire and neglect by the lumber companies. Possessing no logging, farming, or woods skills, Schels was the typical "greenhorn." But what Schels lacked in skill he more than made up for with ambition and a willingness to work hard.

He found his way to north-central Wisconsin and took a job working on the Wolf River Mink and Fur Farm. The owner of the farm was notorious for taking advantage of Chicago boys down on their luck—working them hard before accusing them of stealing in order to get them sent back to the city without a dime of pay.[2] Schels learned of the dirty tricks but wasn't one to be intimidated. He was a hard worker—clearing land with hand tools, cutting trees into firewood in the heat of July and August, and mixing endless barrels of mink feed. He worked for only room and board—oatmeal for breakfast every day and an old steel cot in the attic to sleep on. Though he knew he wasn't being treated fairly, he stuck it out, too proud to go home. The hard work made him stronger and more independent.

"The environment, responsibility and hardships I had while with the mink farmer certainly were gradually forcing me on my own," he wrote.[3]

After two years at the mink farm Schels knew it was time to move on. He moved in with a neighbor, an "old-time Kentucky farmer," to help with chores. It wasn't long before Schels had the opportunity to strike out on his own. The farmer's son-in-law owned some land on nearby Stella Lake and offered Schels a dollar a day to clear shoreline brush. The best part of the offer was that Schels could live in the twelve-by-twelve-foot shack on the property.

"This was really something," wrote Schels, "here the first time in my life doing my own cooking, washing dishes, etc."[4]

The winter of 1933–1934 would be the first on his own and when he really began to live from the land. Using money loaned by his uncle back in Chicago, Schels purchased winter supplies as well as a few leghold traps from the Montgomery Ward catalog. At the time, trapping was one of the few ways to earn hard cash in the north. According to Schels, at that time weasels brought up to fifty cents each, muskrats averaged sixty-five cents, and mink might fetch as much as seven dollars.[5]

"I knew practically nothing about trapping," wrote Schels. "However if one works at it long enough once in a while you catch something."[6]

Schels learned quickly, and by spring he had taken eighteen muskrats, a few weasels, and two mink. The fur was shipped to Montgomery Ward for sale.

With the hard cash made from fur trapping he ordered a Remington .25–20 from the Ward's catalog, his first real gun. "This was always considered a violators gun," wrote Schels. "It had all the firepower needed but the main thing was it didn't make a lot of noise."[7]

Due to low numbers of furbearers, trapping was highly regulated at the time, and much of Schels's fur trapping activity was illegal. However, there was a Depression-era economy in northern Wisconsin in the early '30s. Times were hard, and people did what they could—legal or illegal—to earn hard cash or put food on the table. "So, like all the violating, it would start before season opened and when one is young you are not afraid doing what I considered a little violating," wrote Schels.[8]

By his second winter of trapping Schels had acquired many more traps, including the larger No. 4 Newhouse, a trap big enough for beaver. Schels's trapping skills developed quickly, but skill in avoiding the law lagged behind. "Of course I didn't know that there were other violators around," wrote Schels. "I never saw them but they saw me."[9] Someone, probably another trapper, reported Schels to the game warden. Eventually he got caught with illegal muskrat pelts and spent twenty-seven days in the Oneida County jail as a result.

However, Schels was developing a passion for fur trapping that the law couldn't stop. To be sure, a large part of the lure was the money that could be made, but trapping was becoming something more than a simple quest for economic security. "If anything can get in your blood, it is trapping," he wrote.[10]

Winter beaver trapping was illegal in those days, but it was the beaver pelts that could really bring in some hard cash. Although the big rodents were increasing in all parts of the north in the 1930s, they were still strongly protected by the state.

Beaver trapping was a game of cat and mouse between the trapper and the conservation warden, but Schels soon learned how to expertly play. As did other outlaw beaver trappers, Schels trapped deep in the forest, far from roads and towns, and stayed out in the woods for weeks at a time. "Very seldom did beaver trappers get caught."

"At one time the warden waited twelve days for me to come out as they heard I was in there," wrote Schels.[11]

The illegal beaver couldn't be sold through Montgomery Ward. "There were only a few fur buyers around dealing with illegal beaver skins so at a certain place on a certain night as many as six trappers would come with their furs to meet the buyer there," wrote Schels.[12]

In 1937 Schels took his trapping to a new level. The owner of a resort in the northern Minnesota border country wilderness tempted Schels to head to northern Minnesota. There were thousands of cords of spruce pulpwood for Schels to log if he were to establish a logging camp there.

Schels headed to the wilderness with a crew of Wisconsin boys and built a small logging camp on the Gunflint Trail. The land was different from that in Wisconsin—harsh, rugged terrain and punishing weather. It was too much for the crew, and they headed back to Wisconsin, leaving Schels bankrupt and alone in the northern Minnesota wilderness.

Schels might have given up, too, if it hadn't been for his love of trapping beaver. The resort owner also was an outlaw beaver trapper, and he took Schels deep into the wilderness on a winter trapping expedition. It was an experience that almost killed him, several times.

Schels had come a long way since 1930, but trapping in the unforgiving Superior country was a new game. The trappers packed fifty miles into the wilderness, each carrying an eighty-pound pack. Shortly after Schels made a base camp, his feet and legs became painfully inflamed, the result of boots laced too tight, and he was unable to walk for days. To compound the problem he also developed snow blindness, with painful, raw eyes. He was at the mercy of his partner, who cared more about beaver pelts than he did about a helpless green-horn. Schels tended his own ailments and began to recover.

Retreat was not in Schels's nature. Instead, he struck out on his own, an incredible decision seeing as he had no map and had never trapped the country before. He made his own camp, a thin tent held against a natural rock wall that reflected heat, with balsam boughs to cover the ground.

"When darkness of night surrounds one and you hear the sound of the wind, the trees cracking loud like a shotgun when the temperature gets down below zero, what such a small shelter against this rock wall means on nights like this cannot be counted in dollars and cents," wrote Schels.[13]

When it came time to leave the wilderness with his beaver pelts, Schels again faced a life-or-death situation—he was fifty miles from his cabin and had no map, only a memory in his head of a map he had seen that showed the canoe route he needed to find.

Temperatures dropped to thirty below and colder as he walked in the direction he thought would take him home. Approaching the outlet of a lake, he fell through the ice, snowshoes on his feet and heavy pack on his back. To make matters worse, a winter storm was building. Luckily the water was shallow and he was able to chop his way to shore with a hatchet. A quickly made fire and some dry clothes saved his life. For the next two days he fought hunger, extreme cold, and weariness. Near total collapse, Schels hit the main road at about midnight of the fourth day of travel.

The Minnesota experience solidified his passion for trapping. "Trapping became the backbone of my life no matter how complicated it got," he wrote.[14]

Schels returned to Wisconsin and eventually settled near Eagle River, married, and built a successful lumber business. He continued to trap throughout his life.

Carl Schels died in 1996 at the age of ninety. His book *A Trapper's Legacy* remains a fascinating account of his early years in northern Wisconsin.

Marv Kaukl holding a tame pine marten Courtesy of the author

Chapter 22
Remembering the
State Fur Farm

T hey are gone now. Bill Osburn, Kenny Mills, the Millard brothers, and the others. The men that dedicated their lives to the operation of one of the most unique but little remembered programs of the old Wisconsin Conservation Department.

Marv "Koke" Kaukl retired from the Wisconsin Department of Natural Resources (DNR) in 1984, after forty years of service to the state. He spent his long career working at the state game farm located near Poynette, Columbia County. A year after joining the game farm staff in 1944, Kaukl was assigned to the fur plant, a section of the game farm dedicated to the propagation of native furbearers. He passed away in 2004.

"I'm the last one left," said Kaukl with a mix of pride and sadness. "Not many people today even know about the fur program, not even those here in Poynette."[1]

Today, the facility once known as the Experimental Game and Fur Farm is simply called the State Game Farm, and its focus is pheasants, producing thousands annually to be released on public hunting grounds. When Kaukl was hired, the fur farm section of the facility was a hub of activity with a variety of active projects involving furbearers including mink, fox, raccoon, muskrat, otter, and even pine marten—all part of the state's furbearer research and propagation programs.

"I started at the game farm in May 1944 and transferred to the fur farm that October," said Kaukl. "At that time there was a genetics mink ranch, fox ranch, raccoon propagation ranch, and disease control ranch. I was in charge of the animals at the mink ranch but helped out in the other areas as well."[2]

The Poynette facility was established in 1934 when Harley Mackenzie, chief of the Conservation Commission, combined the existing state game farm operations, which had primarily been located at Peninsula State Park in Door

County with a satellite facility on the Waupun Prison grounds (where prisoners provided labor to hatch and rear game birds from eggs shipped from Door County), into one major facility located just outside Poynette in Columbia County. A third facility, the Moon Lake state game farm, which operated on land leased from the Milwaukee chapter of the Izaak Walton League in Fond du Lac County, continued to operate. Labor to build the new facility came from Civilian Conservation Corps (CCC) and Works Progress Administration (WPA) programs.

The fur section was an integral part of the game farm from the start. Prior to the construction of the new game farm, the conservation department had already been involved in a raccoon stocking program.

A biennial report from the State Conservation Commission stated: "The conservation department is co-operating with the Wisconsin Raccoon Hunters' Association in its raccoon stocking programs. Approximately 20 raccoons were furnished the association in each year of the biennium. A greatly enlarged raccoon stocking program is contemplated for 1933 and 1934, in co-operation with the association."[3]

Although the propagation and stocking of game birds such as pheasants, Hungarian partridge, quail, and chukars was of great importance at the new facility, research into the propagation and care of furbearers, and programs to restock furbearers in the wild, were of equal importance. At the time, there was strong political and economic support to assist the fur farm industry and to provide hunters and trappers with increased opportunities to take furbearers.

Fur farming was big business in Wisconsin in the 1920s, '30s and '40s. By the 1920s, Wisconsin, along with Michigan and Minnesota, was producing half of the nation's commercial fur, and by the 1940s Wisconsin had twice as many fur farms as any other state.[4] One of these farms was the large and highly successful Fromm Bros. ranch, which by the 1930s was reported to be the largest fur farming operation in the world.[5] The Fromm ranch was renowned for its breeding of silver fox. In 1936 *Time* magazine reported: "the Fromm's have 2,000 foxes running wild on their ranch near Wausau, another 4,000 in breeding dens on a ranch near Milwaukee. The 6,000 foxes are valued at about $1,500,000."[6]

The purpose of the fur farm was made clear in the 1933–1934 biennium report from the commission:

Construction began late in the biennium on the experimental fur farm at Poynette, adjoining the state game farm at that site. A modern fur plant, including laboratory, is planned.

The purpose of the fur farm [is] twofold:

(1) to produce annually for stocking from 500 to 1,000 raccoon and from 25 to 50 silver and blue foxes for experimental stocking purposes.

(2) to carry on experimental work at the farm which will consist principally in the attempted breeding and rearing of the rarer furbearing animals such as fisher, marten, and otter. Mink will be given special studies in nutrition, housing, and breeding. Some experimental work will be done with fitch. It is hoped to add a herd of karakul sheep to the fur section in the next biennium, together with an experimental project in the production of white-tailed deer from an economic standpoint.

The fur farm laboratory, which is one of the finest in the central west, will be invaluable not only to the fur farmers in the state, but to the state game farm and to commercial game breeders. It will serve in addition as a clearing house for all wild dead game shipped for analysis, particularly those species where death is caused by cyclic disturbances.

Present breeding stock at the farm includes 150 black, gray and cross raccoon; four pairs of silver fox; three pair of blue fox; two pairs of red fox; one pair of fisher; three pairs of fitch; and one pair of nutria.[7]

There were many disease, genetic, and nutritional problems at commercial fur farms, and research projects through the years at the game farm attempted to solve some of these, much as an agricultural experiment station. Researchers and veterinarians in the disease section worked on projects to study encephalitis in raccoons as well as distemper and rabies in mink and fox. According to Kaukl, an effective distemper vaccine was produced by veterinarians at the farm.

In other projects, fox and mink were scientifically crossed and bred to develop more valuable furs for ranchers, and artificial breeding was attempted. Some studies looked at nutritional requirements of captive animals, as fur farmers were always seeking cost-effective ways to feed their animals. A carp-feeding project looked at ways to utilize carp as mink feed.

Due in part to the influence of organized raccoon hunting groups, raccoons were a prominent feature at the fur farm in the early years. A 1935 visitors guide to the game farm explained the raccoon program: "Raccoon are being reared on a wholesale basis for distribution in the natural 'coon country," the guide stated. "Most of the raccoon which are being released are black raccoon, which when crossed with the native gray variety, produces a superior grade of pelt. This program of release and providing favorable conditions for the natural increase of furbearers will aid many farmer boys who count upon trapping to assist them in financing themselves at school or even at home."[8]

"The raccoon ranch was run by the Millard brothers," said Kaukl. "It was a large facility. At one time I counted over four hundred female coon kept for breeding stock."[9]

Raccoon hunting was extremely popular in the simpler times after the Great Depression, not just because raccoon pelts were a valuable commodity but also due to the numerous field events that could greatly increase the value of a good hound. Although raccoons were not scarce, they were not abundant, and raccoon hunter associations convinced the Conservation Commission to breed and release raccoons for sport hunters.

According to Kaukl the raccoon program was funded by sportsman dollars at first, but the funding shifted to an occupational tax of twenty-five cents per raccoon pelt sold. Eventually the funding came directly from the Wisconsin Raccoon and Fox Hunters Association.

"It was a costly program," said Kaukl. "But it had a lot of support from an influential state senator and a newspaper editor, both involved with the 'coon and fox hunters association."

The support was strong enough to keep the raccoon ranch running at Poynette for twenty years. When it finally shut down in the late 1950s the ranch had produced as many as one thousand animals a year for stocking. The young raccoons were crated up and distributed to wardens for release into the wild.

"A problem with the program was that the raccoon born in spring were released in August. Too young to fend for themselves I thought," said Kaukl. "Many of us at the farm were opposed to the raccoon ranch."[10]

Kaukl was involved in other interesting fur programs at the game farm, including the state's involvement in the fur trade. "Trappers working the state's portion of the Horicon Marsh had to split their take with the state," said Kaukl. "It was a three-to-one split, with the state getting a one-fourth share of the take." The pelts were sent to the game farm where they were graded by Kaukl and put up for auction. An old fur grader named Steve Collins taught Kaukl the art of grading furs. "Beavers were pretty good money back then," Kaukl said. "We averaged about eighteen dollars, with blankets [large pelts] going for forty to forty-five dollars. That was a lot of money in those times."[11]

Another of Kaukl's responsibilities involved maintaining the game farm's live animal exhibits, and his affinity for furbearers won him some notoriety.

In November 1954 *Wisconsin State Journal* staff writer John Newhouse wrote of Kaukl's ability to tame two badgers:

> If there ever was a fighting animal, it's the squat, powerful badger.
>
> And it's extremely rare when one is tamed, for badgers don't cotton much to mankind.
>
> That's why the seasoned animal men at the state game farm here are impressed with the job that Marvin (Koke) Kaukl is doing at the farm with a pair of badgers approaching maturity.[12]

Through the years the fur programs at the game farm were discontinued, with little remaining by the early 1960s. With the modern-day decline of the fur farm industry and the explosion in raccoon numbers in the wild, the old fur programs of the state game farm speak of a different era. All that remains today of the once-vital fur section are concrete foundations of buildings long ago torn down, overgrown with woods and brush, and Marv Kaukl's memories.

Indian Agency House—Portage, Wisconsin WHi Image ID 42764

Chapter 23
"Le Portage" and the Fox-Wisconsin Waterway

Living in a northern Wisconsin river town, I frequently get caught up in the history of the old white pine lumbering days, when shanty boys and river pigs populated the northwoods. Armed with axes and crosscut saws, peaveys and cant hooks, the lumberjacks converted the vast old-growth pines into logs that eventually became lumber to fuel America's growth in the second half of the nineteenth century.

This history is relatively recent and close at hand. The white pine logging era lasted until the early 1900s in some parts of the north. It's easy to find remnants of those days in and around the towns that lumbering built. In some locations on northern public forestlands it is still possible to find the old, gray, decomposing stumps of virgin white pine or hemlock felled during the early logging days.

It's also easy to forget that another hugely important industry left its mark on Wisconsin history: the fur trade—at one time one of the largest commercial enterprises in the world. The fur trade was an industry that, as with lumbering, was full of incredible peril and hardship. The North American fur trade began centuries before the first old-growth northern Wisconsin white pines were felled by the logger's ax.

I was reminded of Wisconsin's role in the development and expansion of the fur trade one day during the summer when I finally had the opportunity to take a side trip off Highway 51 near Portage, Columbia County, and visit the Indian Agency House. I had passed the signs promoting the historic site for years while on my way to somewhere else, always in a hurry. One day, traveling by myself and finding a little time on my hands, I pulled off the highway and followed the small signs leading to the place.

I had a hazy idea in my mind that Portage was an important place geographically because the headwaters of the Fox River came pretty close to the Wisconsin

River there, and Indians and early fur traders had used a portage, or trail, between the two rivers as the final leg of a journey from the Great Lakes to the Mississippi River watershed. I hadn't realized just how important the portage really was until I stopped at the Indian Agency House and began to learn about the hundreds of years of history that were made there.

The Indian Agency House was built in 1832 very near the Fox-Wisconsin portage and across the Fox River from Fort Winnebago.[1] Major David E. Twiggs and three companies of United States infantry had begun construction of the fort four years earlier to protect the portage itself, enabling travelers and traders to safely move from the Great Lakes via Green Bay, up the Fox River, across the portage, and down the Wisconsin River to the Mississippi.[2] The necessity of a fort at the portage was due to a short-lived but bloody conflict between settlers and the Ho-Chunk (Winnebago), known as the Red Bird Uprising, which had ended in 1827 after the surrender of Ho-Chunk chief Red Bird, the uprising's leader.[3]

The Indian Agency House was built as a residence for the first Indian agent at Fort Winnebago, John Kinzie, and his wife, Juliette. Kinzie had been an agent of the American Fur Company and was selected to become the region's first Indian agent because of his familiarity with Indian culture and his ability to speak several Native American languages.[4] His primary role at the agency was to administer the U.S. government's treaty obligations after the close of conflict with the Ho-Chunk and to serve as a mediator in local disputes and conflicts.[5]

Kinzie first arrived at Fort Winnebago in 1829 and probably stayed in one of the crude cabins built there.[6] The adventurous Juliette, whom Kinzie married in 1830, accompanied her husband to the fort shortly after their wedding.[7]

The Kinzies traveled from Green Bay to Fort Winnebago by way of the Fox River. The expedition to the fort was probably a colorful affair, as the Kinzie party included soldiers, French-Canadian voyageurs, and an Indian guide.

In her historically important book about her experiences at Fort Winnebago, *Wau-Bun, The Early Day in the Northwest*, Juliette Kinzie described the boat that would take them to their new home: "It was a moderate-sized Mackinac boat, with a crew of soldiers, and our own three voyageurs in addition, that lay waiting for us—a dark looking structure of some thirty feet in length. Placed in the centre was a framework of slight posts, supporting a roof of canvas, with curtains of the same, which might be let down at the side and ends, after the manner of a country stage-coach, or rolled up to admit light and air."[8]

After arriving at the fort, the couple lived for a time in a rough log building that had served as temporary barracks for soldiers.[9] The structure had been moved to near where the Indian Agency House was eventually built. Juliette described it as having "a very rough and primitive appearance."[10] Finally, in November 1832 the "comfortable dwelling" that had been promised to the Kinzies by the government was completed. The Indian Agency House was a well-built two-story structure with spacious and comfortable rooms, a fitting place for the fine furniture, including a piano, that Juliette had brought with her from the east.

Unfortunately, Juliette enjoyed the new house for only eight months. While John and Juliette were interacting with the Indian tribes of the Wisconsin frontier, the Kinzie family (John's widowed mother and his brothers and sisters) was establishing a claim to 102 acres along the Chicago River near Lake Michigan in the burgeoning settlement of Chicago.[11] John Kinzie resigned his position with the government in order to move to Chicago to help with the subdividing and sale of the property—the geographic center of what would become one of the largest cities in the nation.[12] On July 1, 1833, the Kinzies left the Indian Agency House and Fort Winnebago, never to return.

Remarkably, the Indian Agency House has survived through more than 170 years and still sits on its original foundation, accurately restored and impeccably maintained by the National Society of Colonial Dames of America since the 1930s.

The American presence at the Fox-Wisconsin portage is just one relatively recent chapter in the portage's long and colorful history.

Though Native Americans had utilized the portage for untold millennia, the portage was first "discovered" by Europeans in 1673 when missionary Pierre Marquette and explorer, trader, and trapper Louis Joliet became the first recorded non-natives to traverse the two-mile link between watersheds.

After "annexing" the Upper Great Lakes region in 1671, the French increased efforts to explore the vast territory that they were claiming. With the goal of locating a route to the Great River, the Mississippi, Marquette and Joliet set out in 1673 with a commission from the governor of Quebec. With five companions in two birch bark canoes, the explorers traveled down Lake Michigan to the French post at Green Bay and then up the Fox River to the Mascoutin Indian village, which at that time marked the farthest west of French exploration in Wisconsin.[13]

In his journal of the expedition, Marquette describes their travel through the Fox River to the portage:

> We knew that, at three leagues from Maskoutens, was a river which discharged into Missisipi [sic]. We knew also that the direction we were to follow in order to reach it was west-southwesterly. But the road is broken by so many swamps and small lakes that it is easy to lose one's way, especially as the river leading thither is so full of wild oats [wild rice] that it is difficult to find the channel. For this reason we greatly needed our two guides, who safely conducted us to a portage of 2,700 paces, and helped us transport our canoes to enter that river; after which they returned home, leaving us alone in this unknown country, in the hands of Providence.[14]

Their traversing of the Fox-Wisconsin waterway, the first use of "Le Portage" by Europeans, was an enormous step toward French exploration and domination of the Mississippi River watershed. The narrow, swampy strip of land became increasingly important in the fur trade, as it allowed the French greater access to western fur trading regions—many a voyageur reached the Mississippi by way of the Fox-Wisconsin route.

The fur trade was big business, and it fueled intense competition among European nations with colonial designs on North America. European powers played out global conflicts and quest for empire in the woods and waters of North America. The British, in particular, were fighting for their share of the lucrative fur trade. The oftentimes bloody conflicts between the French and British, collectively known as the French and Indian Wars, promoted alliances between various Indian tribes and rival European powers and greatly influenced the use of the Fox-Wisconsin portage.

In the midst of hostilities, beaver pelts poured into Montreal, the result of so many young men of New France being lured into the fur trade by profits and the prospect of alliances with Indian women.[15] In an attempt to reign in the growing glut of pelts and declining profits, the French suspended the beaver trade in the Great Lakes and canceled the issuance of trading licenses in 1696.[16]

At the end of trade restrictions in 1715, the French greatly expanded their presence, building ten new fur posts in the Western Great Lakes.[17] However, continued conflict with Wisconsin's Fox Indians hampered France's successes.

The Fox had fled their original homeland in Michigan and settled along the Fox River between the portage and Lake Winnebago in the mid-1600s.[18] It was in Wisconsin that they became a powerful force.

The independent Fox, antagonistic to the French, took advantage of their position on the Fox River by endeavoring to obtain complete control of the waterway.[19] The formidable warriors basically closed the Fox-Wisconsin trade route to the French by the 1690s and charged heavy tolls to any adventurous, illegal fur trader who dared to pass through Fox territory.[20]

Closure of the Fox-Wisconsin trade route necessitated the establishment of alternative routes to the Mississippi by the French, leading to the development of routes originating from Lake Superior.[21] However, portages were control points for the waterborne commerce that the fur trade depended on, and the French would not stand for Fox interference. Years of bloody and savage war between the Fox and the French began in 1712 and degenerated into a war of genocide, with the complete annihilation of the Fox an official French objective.[22]

After a French massacre of the Fox in which more than five hundred men, women, and children were killed in 1730, the once proud and strong Fox were destroyed, their numbers just a shadow of what they once had been.[23] Fur traders could once again use the Fox-Wisconsin waterway in relative safety.

French domination of the fur trade was in a decline after the Fox Wars, as Britain began to make inroads into the Great Lakes fur trade.[24] After the conquest of New France by Britain and the signing of a peace treaty in 1763, the Fox-Wisconsin portage passed to British control.

British, French, and Indian traders used the Fox portage all through the time period of the American Revolution. Although no battles were fought there during the Revolution, in 1780 a contingent of British soldiers traveled via the Fox portage en route to attack the Spanish settlement of St. Louis.[25] The soldiers spent several days in the area preparing for the expedition. The attack was repulsed.

Some years later another British military operation, this one directed against Americans, utilized the Fox-Wisconsin waterway to reach the Wisconsin River. After the Revolution and up until the end of the War of 1812, the far-flung frontier outposts in Wisconsin were only nominally under the control of the United States. When the Americans built a small fort at Prairie du Chien in 1814, the British assembled a force of 120 soldiers and 150 Indian allies to capture it.[26]

Leaving Green Bay in June, the largest military force to move through the portage since the French regime floated down the Wisconsin to successfully take the fort.[27]

The War of 1812 eventually led to the establishment of American rule in the Old Northwest permanently, and the Fox portage passed firmly to American control. To maintain its control in Wisconsin, the United States built forts, including Fort Howard at Green Bay and Fort Crawford at Prairie du Chien in 1816.[28]

Twelve years later construction began on Fort Winnebago, bringing us back to the time of John and Juliette Kinzie and the Indian Agency House. However, Kinzie's era really signaled the end of the frontier in Wisconsin. As lead mining displaced the fur trade as Wisconsin's chief industry in the early 1800s, European immigrants poured into the state. A little more than a decade after Kinzie's tenure at Portage, Wisconsin became the thirtieth state of the Union.

Today, the Indian Agency House may be the best-preserved fragment of the vast history of the Fox-Wisconsin portage, and it is well worth a visit. From the front yard of the house, one can look toward the old portage trail and easily imagine the black-robed French missionaries, explorers, voyageurs, fur traders, Indian warriors, British soldiers, and American settlers that once traversed the two-mile link between rivers over the course of two centuries.

Wisconsin deer hunters, late 1800s WHi Image ID 1930

Chapter 24
Pioneer Bits and Pieces

While researching articles for this book, I frequently came across interesting tidbits of Wisconsin sporting history that don't warrant a full story but are interesting little slices of a long past Wisconsin. In the early 1900s newspapers across the state frequently ran stories about the earliest of Wisconsin pioneers and their hunting and fishing memories.

Fishing with Jackson

While many of us are familiar with the Wisconsin fishing experiences of U.S. presidents such as Dwight Eisenhower and Calvin Coolidge, I ran across another interesting connection between Wisconsin and presidential fishing pursuits.

In 1906, the *Appleton Crescent* ran a story about a local woman who, besides having the distinction of being the first woman in Appleton to ride in the first covered carriage (an import from Massachusetts), was also lucky enough to have been a fishing companion of the seventh president of the United States, Andrew Jackson—hero of the Battle of New Orleans in the War of 1812.

As a child, Elizabeth Mereness (née Kling) lived on a farm located very near Sharron Springs, a health resort in New York frequented by southerners, including Jackson, who were escaping oppressive southern summer temperatures. Mereness first met Jackson in the summer of 1833. The former president took a liking to Elizabeth and her sister Eveline and frequently fished with the two girls on a five-acre pond at the Kling farm. The girls dug worms for Jackson, and he always gave the fish he caught to them.[1]

An early Appleton-area settler, Mereness was seventy-seven years old when interviewed by the *Crescent* reporter. She recalled that Jackson "looked as much like the typical picture of 'Uncle Sam' as you could imagine. His hat was shaped just like Uncle Sam's. It was an old grey hat, dirty and greasy in the front.

His face was the same long, thin one which appears in histories."[2]

Jackson continued to spend summers at Sharron Springs and frequent the Kling farm. He died in 1845 at the age of seventy-eight.

Early Madison Hunting

In 1923 the *Madison Capital Times* carried the hunting and fishing reminiscences of an early settler known only as the "Early Madisonian":

> In 1845 Madison was a small hamlet standing in a forest thicket. There were no streets or walks. Prairies and groves, as yet unmarked by evidences of man's presence in the surrounding country, reached to the edges of the lakes. But game was plentiful and fishing most successfully carried on.
>
> Prairie chickens were shot on the capitol square, and quail also filled the game bag. Rabbits were plentiful. An hour's fishing would often give a boatload of finny beauties to be divided among neighbors by the angler.
>
> Deer were numerous, and from the cabin doorway or window, could often be shot. The last one killed on the town site was an old buck, who had become so wise he eluded his fate for several years.
>
> Bear were common at this period, and wolves innumerable. The latter became so troublesome that an official wolf-catcher was engaged.
>
> Prairie fires annually crossed the site from one marsh to another, passing through the timber between Capitol Park and Fourth Lake. Unquestionably a good deal of what may be called smaller game perished in the flames. But wild duck and geese escaped—either by high flight or by early migration southward, and each returning spring brought the blackbirds and pigeons as excellent foundations for pot pie.[3]

Oldest Hunter in Superior

G. J. Anderson of Solon Springs, touted as Douglas County's oldest deer hunter by the *Superior Telegram* in November 1914, provided his early hunting memories to a *Telegram* reporter.

Anderson told the reporter "how he had shot the first deer killed by him in Douglas County in November 1880, on the site where the Hotel Superior now stands."[4]

"I never thought then that I was standing on what would be in a comparatively short time the busiest corner in a large city," reminisced Anderson. "All around me were huge pine trees, and I remember thinking what fine logs they would make."[5]

Anderson was an old man when he was interviewed, but he confidently told the reporter, "I'm going to get my venison this year again."[6]

Deer Stacked Like Cordwood

In 1927 the *Superior Telegram* interviewed another area old-timer, Pat Simons. He recalled the market hunting days of the mid-1800s.

"I've seen deer stacked like cordwood as far as from here to that shed, and 20 feet high," Simons told the newspaper. "Fellows made their living that way. They'd go into the woods in the winter and shoot deer and haul them out with teams later. They were shipped to the markets. The deer were thick. One could shoot them from the door of the cabin. Often they would come right into town."[7]

Simons also remembered how the now extinct passenger pigeon existed in huge numbers in the area.

"Partridges were thick around here, and wild pigeons. I've seen the pigeons come down and cover whole trees," he remarked.[8]

Hunting for the Logging Camps

Also in 1927 the *Eau Claire Telegram* interviewed one of the last of the white pine loggers, the fast-disappearing generation of men who had cleared the northern pineries. James D. Terry of Augusta felled trees and drove logs in the Eau Claire and Chippewa Falls area in the 1860s and '70s. He told the reporter that it became his job to supply the lumber camps with venison:

I was to receive four dollars per head for the deer killed, also my board. I had only to show the toters where the deer could be found. I began hunting November first and by January had killed thirty-eight deer and two bear, an old one and a cub. I was paid ten dollars for the large bear and five dollars for the cub.

After January first I began working as a chopper, and in the spring helped drive the logs down to the Five Mile Dam, at what is now Altoona.[9]

Terry spent two winters hunting for the lumber camps.

"Both winters I hunted alone," he remembered. "The gun I used was a double barrel, muzzleloader rifle, about thirty-eight caliber, and was made by Mr. Schlegelmilch senior, the pioneer gunsmith of Eau Claire."[10]

Those early pioneers are all long gone now, but luckily some of their stories were recorded by the newspapers. Wisconsin still has its share of old-time hunters, trappers, and anglers who can fondly recall the Wisconsin outdoors as they existed in the 1930s, '40s, and '50s. It is hoped that their stories will find their way to the archives of history as well.

White Sox President Charles Comiskey (left) and Cubs President Bill Veeck Sr., 1920
Courtesy of the Chicago Historical Society

Chapter 25

Charles Comiskey
and the Northwoods

Referred to as America's "national pastime" since 1856, the game of baseball truly became the most popular organized sport in the country in the early 1900s.[1] The advent of the American League in 1901, the first World Series in 1903, and baseball celebrities such as Ty Cobb, Cy Young, and "Shoeless" Joe Jackson packed fans into stadiums across the country. Promoters began to realize that baseball's popularity with the masses translated into big money. The owners of successful ball clubs were becoming wealthy and powerful. Charles A. Comiskey, owner of the 1906 World Champion Chicago White Sox, was no exception.

Comiskey, known as the "Old Roman" because of his statuesque profile, demonstrated his wealth and prestige by sponsoring a grand pilgrimage to the Wisconsin northwoods shortly after the close of each baseball season. Comiskey's entourage would include prominent men from the world of baseball, such as American League commissioner Ban Johnson and Dubuque, Iowa, baseball magnate Tom Loftus as well as an array of well-connected politicians, judges, lawyers, and business moguls. Numerous members of the press also accompanied the autumn expedition, which could number sixty people or more.[2] The stated purpose of the northern ventures, which began as early as 1903, was to relax and unwind after the hectic baseball season and engage in a little hunting and fishing.

Comiskey's first northern Wisconsin camp was located near Springstead, in Iron County, thirty-five miles from the nearest railroad station in Fifield.[3] Provisions were hauled by wagon for several days prior to the party's arrival each fall. At camp, some of the most prominent men in America at the time spent northern Wisconsin autumn days on the water in pursuit of musky or tromping the woods with shotguns in hand.

Nights at camp were spent in lighthearted revelry and hunting camp camaraderie. Practical jokes were common, as were mock court proceedings for those who broke the camp "rules," such as missing a meal or snoring during the night. Sportswriter and early Comiskey biographer G. W. Axelson wrote: "These were conducted according to Hoyle, as there were always enough bona fide judges and lawyers in the party to assure even-handed justice."[4]

In 1907 the camp at Springstead was abandoned for a new recreational property a few miles to the north. Comiskey purchased a large tract of land on Trude Lake, twelve miles from the village of Mercer. A large and elegant log lodge was built on the property, as were several smaller cabins.

The *Rhinelander New North* listed some of Comiskey's entourage in a 1910 newspaper report: "Those in the party beside Mr. Comiskey were B. B. Johnson, president of the American league; C. C. Spink, St. Louis editor; James McAleer, manager of the Washington team; Jack Sheridan, veteran umpire; George Thompson of the Lake Shore railroad; P. F. McCarthy, Jas. McTauge of St. Louis; Bob Walsh, Tom Miller, Pete Lamler, Al. Hayden, Jimmy McLain, Eddie Welsh and Joe Farrell, Chicago nimrods of note."[5]

The Rhinelander Daily News reported on the Comiskey entourage passing through town in 1912: "Those who were at the Northwestern depot Tuesday morning when the limited train went north had the opportunity of seeing through the car windows many of the most noted personages in the world of baseball. The White Sox players Chicago's Champions headed by Charles Comiskey passed through the city on their way to their annual outing at Camp Jerome, Trude Lake, near Mercer."[6]

Comiskey developed the Jerome Club into a premier hunting and fishing camp. Eventually consisting of six hundred acres of land, the entire property was enclosed by a sixteen-foot-high woven wire fence.[7] Comiskey indulged his love for wildlife by releasing a variety of animals into the enclosure, including deer, elk, moose, antelope, and buffalo. Many of the animals were fairly tame, having been raised at camp, and provided camp visitors with great entertainment.

One of the most famous animals at the Jerome Club was "Big Bill" the moose. "Bill was captured in the Rainy Lake region while still wobbling," wrote G. W. Axelson. "He was brought up on a bottle at Camp Jerome and in time grew up to become one of the most magnificent antlered specimens on the continent."[8]

Unfortunately, Bill's magnificence came to an abrupt end. "One night during a storm, a fallen tree leveled a section of the fence. Bill found the hole and struck out for the land of his nativity," wrote Axelson.[9] Before Comiskey, who had offered a five hundred dollar reward for the safe return of the moose, could recapture Bill, a local hunter shot him.

A second moose met a similar fate. This moose was named "Red" in honor of Red Faber, a popular White Sox pitcher at the time and future Baseball Hall of Famer.

"Charles Comiskey has lost another big moose from his private game preserve on Trude Lake near Mercer," a northwoods newspaper reported in September 1916. "The animal strayed away from the preserve through a gate, which had been left open by some careless visitor, and was later killed when he attempted to run down a young man walking along a railroad track."[10]

The report went on to detail the incident:

The animal had wandered west from the river until it reached Roddis L. & V. Company's logging railroad a mile northwest of Agenda about six o'clock in the evening. At the same time three of the Lawler boys, Attley, Ted and Basil, were looking for their father's cows in this vicinity. Basil, the youngest of the boys, heard a crashing in the woods near him and went to investigate, thinking the noise was made by one of the cows. Instead of a mild-tempered cow, however, he found himself confronted by no other than 'Reddy,' who had a look of envy in its eye, though this interesting fact was to the lad unknown. He had barely time to realize that the largest animal he had ever seen, with wide, flat horns, was standing before him, when the animal came towards him.[11]

Young Basil was able to jump across the tracks just before an approaching train and the big moose went back into the woods.

A short time later one of Basil's older brothers, Attley, encountered the moose on the railroad tracks and was also pursued by the big animal. Attley, however, was in possession of a rifle and fired three shots at the moose, killing it.

The arrival of Comiskey and his band of notables to the lakeland region each fall caused great excitement in local communities and was usually well reported by the local press.

"Fifty adherents of the world's champion White Sox of Chicago are encamped at Camp Jerome at Trude Lake, west of Mercer as the guests of President Comiskey of the Chicago American League club, states the *Hurley Miner*," reported the *Rhinelander New North* in November 1917. "Three special sleepers were attached to the Northwestern train to accommodate the celebrants. They were cut off at Mercer to permit the party to disembark preparatory to a twelve mile jaunt in to the woods, where the Jerome Country club was all lit up in preparation for the annual fall invasion."[12]

The White Sox had recently beaten the New York Giants four games to two in the six-game World Series.

The press sometimes noted, to the disappointment of little boys and adults alike, that Comiskey's party rarely included his champion ballplayers. "President Comiskey, Manager Rowland of the White Sox, and Business Manager Williams of the Cubs were the only baseball celebrities included in the party. The rest of it was composed of White Sox rooters and Chicago baseball scribes. None of the world's champions made the trip, which is expected to include a fortnight's stay in the woods," reported *New North*.[13]

While the Old Roman spared little expense to entertain his well-connected guests, he was famous for his tightfistedness when it came to the players. The poor pay received by White Sox players while the club itself was very profitable, may have led to the famous "Black Sox" scandal of 1919. Eight players were banned from baseball for life after being implicated in throwing the World Series that year for one hundred thousand dollars. However, outright greed was also likely a factor, as the split was more than most professional ballplayers made in a year at that time.

It is unclear whether Comiskey came north that year, as the scandal didn't break until 1920. However, he may have been in the process of selling the Trude Lake estate and moving his base of northern operations to the Eagle River area.

In 1920 Comiskey purchased property on Dam Lake in northern Oneida County. "From the *Eagle River Review* it is learned that Charles Comiskey, owner of the Chicago White Sox and one of the big men in the baseball world, is making extensive improvements to his farm and resort property on Dam Lake."

"Comiskey purchased this estate last spring and it is one of the finest properties in the entire northern Wisconsin lake region," reported *New North*.[14]

The success of Comiskey's deer season also was reported by *New North* that year: "Charles Comiskey, owner of the Chicago White Sox and one of the most notable figures in the realm of baseball, was numbered among the successful deer hunters in Oneida County this season. Enroute from his estate on Dam Lake to Chicago 'the Old Roman' passed through Rhinelander with a fine buck in his possession. Mr. Comiskey acquired his deer after a several days hunt. It was one of the most perfect specimens of buck seen here this year."[15]

Comiskey and his White Sox franchise were never quite the same after the World Series scandal. Shortly afterward, Comiskey became ill and gave up active operation of the team. He continued to spend time in the northwoods at his Dam Lake estate, and it was there that the Old Roman died in 1931 at seventy-two years of age.

"Succumbing to heart and kidney troubles, Charles A. Comiskey, owner of the Chicago White Sox base ball team, passed away Monday morning at his summer home on Dam Lake, northwest of Rhinelander, after a lingering illness of several months. The body was taken Monday night to Chicago for burial," reported the *New North*.[16]

The *New North* noted that "his son, J. Louis Comiskey, was at his bedside when he passed away."[17]

Wisconsin white pine helped to build Cornell University WHi Image ID 2413

Chapter 26
The Wisconsin White Pine That Built a New York University

T raveling through the Wisconsin counties that contain the Upper Chippewa River watershed, from the headwater counties of Ashland and Bayfield down to Chippewa County, one wouldn't observe a lot that speaks to the relationship the vast region once had with a well-known New York university.

Cornell University, located in Ithaca, New York, is one of the country's most prestigious academic institutions. However, few people today—New Yorkers and Wisconsinites alike—realize that Cornell, founded in 1868, owes its success to the virgin white pine that once grew along the Chippewa River and its tributaries.

The story of how a New Yorker intent on establishing an agriculture and mechanical arts college in his hometown was able to realize his dream thanks to the natural resources of northern Wisconsin began in the midst of the Civil War.

While the War Between the States was raging in 1862, the Union government still had to attend to the needs of a growing country, including the ever-increasing demand for institutions of higher learning. Cash strapped but possessing a huge amount of public land, the government often used land grants as an incentive for economic development, such as the establishment of railroads.

A congressman from Vermont, Justin Smith Morrill, proposed to use this same strategy to meet the demand for colleges. The first Morrill Act, also known as the Land Grant College Act of 1862, provided for the distribution of public land to each state—30,000 acres for each congressional seat held by the state. Proceeds from the sale of this land would provide funds for the establishment and support of an "agriculture and mechanic arts" college in each state (known as land-grant colleges).[1] Not all of the states had a sufficient amount of public land within its borders to meet the amount of their land grant, so the act allowed these states to choose public lands in other states.[2] Land was issued in the form of land scrip certificates (one certificate equaled 160 acres of land).

A wealthy New Yorker named Ezra Cornell sensed opportunity in the Morrill Act. New York, as the state with the largest number of delegates in Congress, received scrip for nearly a million acres of public land.[3] Cornell could realize his dream of a college in his hometown of Ithaca if he could somehow direct or control the sale of New York's great land grant.

After some astute political maneuvering, which involved using his personal fortune to purchase land scrip from the state, Cornell was able to gain control of the scrip to ensure it was utilized for Cornell University.[4] While many states were acquiring public lands and quickly disposing of them at current market rates for immediate income, Cornell proceeded slowly, looking toward the west for lands that could produce a better return.

Good fortune visited Cornell when friend and former Ithaca resident William A. Woodward suggested he invest the scrip in the pine lands of Wisconsin. Woodward was in Wisconsin and was witness to the growing lumber and land speculation business there.

According to Paul Wallace Gates, author of *The Wisconsin Pine Lands of Cornell University, a Study in Land Policy and Absentee Ownership*, Cornell's decision to invest the bulk of the New York land grant in Wisconsin was to become "one of the largest and ultimately most successful land speculations in American history."[5]

Speculation in public lands had been a part of the picture in Wisconsin since statehood in 1848. Gates wrote: "By 1865 the public domain in Wisconsin had been reduced to ten or eleven million acres, most of which was in the northern half of the state."[6]

When Ezra Cornell entered the scene in the mid-1800s he became associated with a land agent named Henry C. Putnam of Eau Claire. Putnam was familiar with the region and knew where the most productive tracts of pine were located.[7]

Gates wrote: "Putnam began operations in a big way when told to go ahead and locate Cornell's scrip. He employed land hunters to roam the Chippewa and its tributaries, the Flambeau, the Jump, the Thornapple and the Red Cedar."[8]

By 1867 Cornell had acquired nearly five hundred thousand acres of land in Wisconsin, most of it pine land. Cornell's acquisitions effectively made him and Cornell University "the largest single owner of pine lands in the northwest, aside from the railroads and the governments of Wisconsin and the U.S."[9]

Acquiring the land was just the beginning. To make money for the university, Cornell then had to sell the land. Because he had acquired large tracts of choice pine in very remote areas of the Upper Chippewa, it would take some time and patience for the land's value to increase sufficiently to make good returns.

Although some small land sales were made in the 1860s, Cornell began to see significant sales only in the 1870s. By this time it was clear to university trustees that Ezra Cornell had taken on a bigger project than he was capable of managing. Cornell, according to Gates, "had little conception of the magnitude or complexity of the burden or of the risks he assumed."[10] In 1874 the university trustees, under the direction of lumberman Henry W. Sage, took control of the land operation.[11] Sage, unlike Cornell, was a shrewd judge of pine lands and began to make very profitable sales for the university.

In the early 1880s forces joined to produce a sharp increase in the value of Wisconsin pine lands. A developing scientific forestry-management movement led some to predict that the pine would soon be gone if not better managed.[12] This helped fuel the demand for the remaining pine. At this same time the U.S. economy was pulling itself out of a recession and the lumber business was good.

Sage made a sale to the lumber company Weyerhaeuser that netted the university $1,841,746.[13] A sale to lumber company Knapp-Stout in 1880 netted $477,550.[14] Cornell stumpage sales in 1887 totaled $746,461.[15] By 1893 most of the valuable Cornell land had been sold.

According to Cornell University: "When all of the timber and land had been sold and the administration of the Western lands was closed in 1935, the university had generated a gross of $6.8 million and a net of $5.1 million. While New York had received one tenth of the 1862 land grant, the University's management of the scrip yielded one third of the total grant revenues generated by all the states."[16] By comparison, Wisconsin had received a 240,000-acre land grant that netted the University of Wisconsin about $300,000.[17]

Gates wrote: "Otherwise the Badger state has forgotten the connection it once had with the institution at Ithaca. Cornell alumni, students and faculty, on the other hand, should cherish the memory of their founding father's wisdom in undertaking the great land venture in Wisconsin . . . nor should they be unaware of the cost of the investment to the state of Wisconsin."[18]

Northeast Wisconsin waterfowlers Courtesy of Neal Lendved

Notes

Chapter 1: Fish Stories

1. "Some Fish Yarn: Three Lakes Has a New One—Can You Beat It?" *The New North*, October 3, 1912.
2. "Man Hooks Pike; Musky Leaps in Boat," *Rhinelander Daily News*, August 28, 1965.
3. "Big Fish Swamps Boat: Two Fishermen Nearly Drown While Trying to Land Musky," *The New North*, August 20, 1914.
4. "Nine Pound Trout Nearly Drowns Angler," *The Wisconsin Sportsman*, June 1937.
5. "Fish Chases Anglers from Their Boat," *The Wisconsin Sportsman*, June 1937.
6. "Fighting Wall Eye Chases Madison Woman from Lake," *The Wisconsin Sportsman*, August 1937.
7. "Killed Big Musky with a Club: And the Slayer Was a Woman, Too, Doing It All Alone," *Wausau Daily Record-Herald*, August 17, 1908.
8. "Fisherwoman Lands Two Fish at a Time," *Wausau Daily Record-Herald*, November 6, 1940.
9. Ed Wodalski, "Ed's Northwoods Notebook: It Got Away," *Rhinelander Daily News*, July 19, 1977.
10. Ed Wodalski, "Ed's Northwoods Notebook: Monster Muskie Resurfaces," *Rhinelander Daily News*, August 2, 1977.

Chapter 2: Boats in the Backyard

1. Laurel Reed Edwards, written communication with the author, February 2010.
2. *Commemorative Biographical Record of the West Shore of Green Bay, Wisconsin Including the Counties of Brown, Oconto, Marinette and Florence* (Chicago: J.H. Beers & Co., 1896), 712.

3. WDNR List of State Parks, www.dnr.state.wi.us/Org/land/parks/specific/ findapark.html#copculture.

4. Claude Jean Allouez, Father Allouez's Journey into Wisconsin 1669–1670, American Journeys Collection, Wisconsin Historical Society, Document No. AJ-048, 146.

5. "Oconto's Early History," *Oconto County Reporter*, June 10, 1909.

6. Ibid.

7. "Oconto, Wisconsin," newspaper article not dated, Wisconsin Historical Society, Wisconsin Local History & Biography Articles.

8. Oconto County Wisconsin Genealogical Project, www.rootsweb.ancestry.com/ ~wioconto/OCRPioneers2.htm.

9. *Commemorative Biographical Record of the West Shore of Green Bay, Wisconsin*, 712.

10. The Swampland Grant Act of 1850 was federal legislation that enabled several states, including Wisconsin, to select verified swamp or overflowed lands from the public domain and have these lands deeded to the state. The purpose of the act was to promote the conversion of swampland to arable agricultural lands. Proceeds from the sale of these lands to private individuals would help recover the costs incurred from drainage projects. However, some states granted the selected lands to railroads, and others used the proceeds to fund educational institutions.

11. Donald "Ducky" Reed, interview with the author, March 2009.

12. Laurel Reed Edwards, written communication with the author, February 2010.

Chapter 3: The Mepps Story

1. Mike Sheldon, interview with the author, September 2001. Unless otherwise noted, information for this chapter was derived from this interview.

Chapter 4: Trouting on the Brule: An 1875 Fishing Expedition to Northern Wisconsin and Michigan

1. John Lyle King, *Trouting on the Brule River: Or Summer-Wayfaring in the Northern Wilderness* (Chicago: Chicago Legal News Co., 1880).

Chapter 5: Lost Outboard Recovered after Seventy Years

1. Dorothy Uthe, interview with the author, October 2002.

2. Peter Hunn, *The Old Outboard Book* (Camden, ME: International Marine, 2002), 82.

3. Ibid., 83.

Chapter 6: Carl Marty's Northernaire: A Special Place in Time

1. August Derleth, *Mr. Conservation: Carl Marty and His Forest Orphans* (Park Falls, WI: MacGregor Litho, Inc., 1971), 1, 13.

2. Ibid., 18.

3. Ibid., 19.

4. Carl Marty Jr., "Northernaire: Built with a Guest's Viewpoint," *Resort Management* (August 1947).

5. Ibid.

6. Ibid.

7. Ibid.

8. Derleth, *Mr. Conservation*, 18.

9. Cappy Gagnon, "Cy Williams," The Baseball Biography Project, http://bioproj.sabr.org.

10. "'46 Tourist Season Prospects Bright," *Rhinelander Daily News*, March 21, 1946.

11. Ibid.

12. Marty, "Northernaire."

13. "Gypsy Rose Lee, Speaks Briefly," *Rhinelander Daily News*, July 11, 1947.

14. Edith Lassen Johnson, *Mother Is a Saint Bernard* (self published, 1970).

15. Derleth, *Mr. Conservation*, 22.

16. Carl Marty, *Northernaire's Ginger and Her Woodland Orphans* (self published, 1953), 12.

17. Derleth, *Mr. Conservation*, 3.

18. Doris Goldsworthy, interview with the author, August 2007.

19. *Northernaire and Showboat News*, no. 1.

20. Ibid.

21. "Town Prepares for Arrival of 'King of Comedy' Bob Hope," *The Three Lakes News*, August 10, 1983.

22. Tom Michele, "New Owners Plan Big Changes for Northernaire," *Rhinelander Daily News*, March 10, 1996.

23. Ibid.

24. "Northernaire to Be Razed," *Rhinelander Daily News*, May 1, 1996.

25. "Northernaire Is Reborn in Three Lakes," *Rhinelander Daily News*, August 14, 2007.
26. "Northernaire Sold to Eau Claire Company," *Rhinelander Daily News*, July 20, 2004.
27. "Northernaire Is Reborn in Three Lakes."

Chapter 7: Hazen's Long Lake Lodge
1. Joel and Janet McClure, interview with the author, July 2003.
2. Ibid.
3. Ibid.

Chapter 8: First Resorts: Teal Lake Lodge
1. Tim Ross, interview with the author, March 2003.
2. Ibid.
3. Teal Lake Lodge History, http://teallakelodge.com/ross'-teal-lake-history
4. Tim Ross, interview with the author, March 2003.
5. Ibid.
6. Ibid.

Chapter 9: Mel's Trading Post
1. Mitch Mode, interview with the author, February 2006.

Chapter 10: Pastika's Sport Shop: Ninety Years of Muskies and Minnows
1. Leon Pastika, interview with the author, October 2006.
2. Ibid.
3. Ibid.
4. Ibid.
5. Ibid.
6. Al Rosenquist, interview with the author, October 2006.

Chapter 11: Duke's Outboards: A Northwoods Institution
1. Peter Hunn, *The Old Outboard Book* (Camden, ME: International Marine, 2002), 15.
2. Ibid., 16.
3. Duke and Dorothy Montgomery, interview with the author, July 2002.

4. Ibid.

5. Hunn, *The Old Outboard Book*, 16.

6. Kris Gilbertson, "Duke Has Kept Up to Date with Motors for the Past 60 Years," *Rhinelander Daily News*, August 2, 1994.

7. Jim Montgomery, interview with the author, July 2002.

Chapter 12: The Rhinelander Boat Company

1. Joy Vancos, interview with the author, June 2002.

2. Ibid.

3. Ibid.

4. Ibid.

5. "Boat Factory Starts: Will Be Busy Throughout the Coming Winter Season," *The New North*, September 21, 1911.

Chapter 13: Waterfowl Hunting with Live Decoys

1. Outdoor Life, *The Story of American Hunting and Firearms* (New York, NY: Sunrise Books/E.P. Dutton & Company, Inc., 1959), 131–132.

2. Ibid., 132.

3. Gordon MacQuarrie, "Minnie the Moocher," in *More Stories of the Old Duck Hunters* (Minocqua, WI: Willow Creek Press, 1990), 35–43.

4. Outdoor Life, *The Story of American Hunting and Firearms*, 132.

5. Philip S. Habermann, Reminiscences, 1988, Wisconsin Historical Society Manuscripts Collection, WIHV89-A115.

Chapter 14: Spring Duck Hunting in the 1800s

1. Louis McLane Hobbins Papers, 1888–1941, Wisconsin Historical Society Manuscripts Collection, WIHV94-A2042.

Chapter 15: An Old Dog for a New Century: The History of the American Water Spaniel

1. David Duffey, "All American Water Spaniels," *Hunting Retriever* (February/March 1986): 6.

2. James B. Spencer, "The American Water Spaniel: Yankee Doodle Dandy," *Wildfowl Magazine* (April/May, 1987): 48.

3. Steve Grooms, "An All-American Gun Dog: The American Water Spaniel," *Fins and Feathers* (May 1975): 39.
4. Duffey, "The Neglected American," 154.
5. Ibid., 152–154.
6. Ibid.
7. John and Mary Barth, interview with the author, January 2000.
8. Spencer, "The American Water Spaniel," 48.
9. John and Mary Barth, interview.

Chapter 16: The Armistice Day Storm: The Winds of Hell
1. Mark Stell, "The Winds of Hell," Minnesota Public Radio, November 10, 2000.
2. "Verage Receives Hunting Laws," *The New North*, September 5, 1940.
3. "Ducks Delayed," *The New North*, November 1940.
4. Stell, "The Winds of Hell."
5. Harold Hettrick, "1940 Armistice Day Storm: Harold Hettrick's Story," recorded as part of "Hunting Stories," a narrative session held as part of the Smithsonian Folklife Festival, July 2, 1998.
6. Stell, "The Winds of Hell."
7. Ibid.
8. Gordon MacQuarrie, "Armistice Day Storm," in *MacQuarrie Miscellany* (Wautoma, WI: Willow Creek Press, 1987), 151.
9. Ibid., 153.
10. Ibid., 151.
11. "Big Eau Pleine Reservoir Searched for Missing Man: Hamburg Farmer on Hunting Trip, Believed Drowned on Monday," *Wausau Daily Record-Herald*, November 13, 1940.
12. Ibid.
13. Ibid.
14. Ibid.
15. "Body of Duck Hunter Found on Eau Pleine Island: Apparently Victim of Exposure; Coroner Conducts Investigation," *Wausau Daily Record-Herald*, November 14, 1940.
16. Associated Press, "Nine Are Dead, Many Missing as Storm Sweeps Wisconsin," *Rhinelander Daily News*, November 12, 1940.
17. Ibid.

18. Ibid.
19. Ibid.
20. Lee Brunner, "Armistice Day 1940," *Wisconsin Sportsman* (November/ December 1974): 20.
21. Ibid.
22. Associated Press, "Searching Parties Hunt More Victims in State: Wisconsin Takes Stock of Losses in Death-Dealing Gale," *Wausau Daily Record-Herald*, November 13, 1940.
23. "At Least Nine Die in State; Several Missing," *Wausau Daily Record-Herald*, November 12, 1940.
24. Neal Lendved, written communication with the author, 2009.
25. Associated Press, "Searching Parties Hunt More Victims in State."
26. "The Storm of November 11, 12 and 13," *The Lightship* (newsletter of the Lake Huron Marine Lore Society) 12, no. 3 (November 1990).
27. "At Least 65 Seamen Feared Drowned in Worst Storm in History of Lake Michigan: Two Huge Freighters Believed to Have Sunk," *Wausau Daily Record-Herald*, November 13, 1940.
28. Michigan Shipwrecks Research Associates, www.michiganshipwrecks.org/ davock.htm.
29. Ibid.
30. Associated Press, "Searching Parties Hunt More Victims in State."
31. National Weather Service Weather Forecast Office: Armistice Day Storm, www.crh.noaa.gov/arx/events/armistice.php.
32. Ibid.
33. Ibid.

Chapter 17: One Day in March 1933

1. Vern Frechette, interview with the author, February 2002.
2. Chick Sheridan, "Ice Rescue Still Subject of Conversation Today," *Ashland Daily Press*, March 31, 1983.
3. "Thrilling Rescues of Men on the Ice: Others Still Sought," *Ashland Daily Press*, March 9, 1933.
4. Ibid.

Chapter 18: Ike's First Vacation to the Wisconsin Northwoods

1. "Eisenhower in Minocqua Today: Chief of Army Arrives on Vacation Trip," *Rhinelander Daily News*, July 15, 1946.
2. "Eisenhower Visit Chief Topic for Minocqua Area," *Rhinelander Daily News*, July 16, 1946.
3. Ibid.
4. "Eisenhower in Minocqua Today."
5. "Eisenhower Visit Chief Topic for Minocqua Area."
6. "Eisenhower in Minocqua Today."
7. "'Ike' Sets Pace for Brothers in Muskie Fishing," *Rhinelander Daily News*, July 18, 1946.
8. Ibid.
9. Kris Gilbertson, "'Ike' Impressed by Cordiality of North: Enjoyed Vacation, He Says in Leaving Area Last Night," *Rhinelander Daily News*, July 22, 1946.
10. Associated Press, "Letter Written to 'Ike' in '45 Pays Off for Badger Girl," *Rhinelander Daily News*, July 19, 1946.
11. Ibid.
12. Gilbertson, "'Ike' Impressed by Cordiality of North."
13. Ibid.
14. Joyce Laabs, *A Collection of Northwoods Nostalgia from the Pages of the "Lakeland Times"* (Sun Prairie, WI: Royle Publishing Co., 1978), 141.
15. Ibid.
16. Dwight D. Eisenhower Library, Howard Young Papers, www.eisenhower .archives.gov/research/finding_aids/PDFs/Young_Howard_Papers.pdf.

Chapter 19: The Summer White House on the Brule

1. Ishbel Ross, *Grace Coolidge and Her Era: The Story of a President's Wife* (New York: Dodd, Mead and Company, 1962), 223.
2. Albert M. Marshall, *Brule Country* (St. Paul, MN: The North Central Publishing Company, 1954), 174.
3. Ibid., 171–172.
4. Ibid., 172.
5. Ibid., 173.
6. Ibid., 175.

7. Ibid.

8. Associated Press, "Brule 'Dressed Up' to Greet the Nation's Chief Executive," June 15, 1928, President Coolidge Brule River scrapbook, Wisconsin Historical Society.

9. Ibid.

10. Ibid.

11. Associated Press, "Rents at Brule Advance Up to 700 Per Cent," June 3, 1928, President Coolidge Brule River scrapbook, Wisconsin Historical Society.

12. Marshall, *Brule Country*, 175.

13. A. B. Kapplin, "President Finds Estate Is Ideal Place to Retire," *Duluth Herald*, 1928, President Coolidge Brule River scrapbook, Wisconsin Historical Society.

14. Ibid.

15. Ross, *Grace Coolidge and Her Era*, 181.

16. Ibid., 230.

17. "Antoine 'Packed' Mails Over Old 92-Mile Trail," President Coolidge Brule River scrapbook, Wisconsin Historical Society.

18. A. I. Darymple, "Chance to Guide President Came Too Late for Old Antoine Dennis," President Coolidge Brule River scrapbook, Wisconsin Historical Society.

19. Ibid.

20. Marshall, *Brule Country*, 178.

21. "Guide Injured, President Tries Trap Shooting," President Coolidge Brule River scrapbook, Wisconsin Historical Society.

22. Reminiscences of Rebekah Knight Cochran, 1978, President Coolidge Brule River scrapbook, Wisconsin Historical Society.

23. Ibid.

24. Marshall, *Brule Country*, 177.

25. Douglas R. Mackenzie, "Brule Claims Coolidges for the Summer," President Coolidge Brule River scrapbook, Wisconsin Historical Society.

26. "Coolidge Devotes First Vacation Day to Fish and Nature," June 16, 1928, President Coolidge Brule River scrapbook, Wisconsin Historical Society.

27. Marshall, *Brule Country*, 177.

28. Kapplin, "President Finds Estate Is Ideal Place to Retire."

29. "Says President Is Good Angler," President Coolidge Brule River scrapbook, Wisconsin Historical Society.
30. A. B. Kapplin, "Canoe Thrills President; Not So Convention," *Duluth Herald*, 1928, President Coolidge Brule River scrapbook, Wisconsin Historical Society.
31. "President Is Spending Last Hours in North," President Coolidge Brule River scrapbook, Wisconsin Historical Society.
32. President Coolidge's Farewell, September 10, 1928, President Coolidge Brule River scrapbook, Wisconsin Historical Society.
33. Reminiscences of Rebekah Knight Cochran.

Chapter 20: Murder at Pelican Lake

1. "Keeler Rites Will Be Held in Enterprise," *Rhinelander Daily News*, December 8, 1931.
2. Ibid.
3. "Violator Killed Enterprise Man?: Farmer Slain; Rodd, Carlson Launch Probe," *Rhinelander Daily News*, December 7, 1931.
4. Ibid.
5. Ibid.
6. Ibid.
7. Ibid.
8. Ibid.
9. Ibid.
10. John Mistely, interview with the author, December 2000.

Chapter 21: Trapping in the Blood: The Carl Schels Story

1. Carl Schels, *A Trapper's Legacy: The Tales of a Twentieth Century Trapper* (Merillville, IN: ICS Books, Inc., 1984), 3.
2. Ibid., 5.
3. Ibid., 6.
4. Ibid., 8.
5. Ibid., 12.
6. Ibid.
7. Ibid., 14.
8. Ibid., 16.

9. Ibid.

10. Ibid., 18.

11. Ibid., 34.

12. Ibid., 51.

13. Ibid., 85.

14. Ibid., 99.

Chapter 22: Remembering the State Fur Farm

1. Marv Kaukl, interview with the author, April 2000.

2. Ibid.

3. Biennial report of the State Conservation Commission of Wisconsin for the fiscal years ending June 30, 1931, and June 30, 1932. Madison: 1932, 89, http://digital.library.wisc.edu/1711.dl/WI.RepConsCom34.

4. Dictionary of Wisconsin History, Fur Farming, http://www.wisconsinhistory.org/dictionary/index.asp.

5. The Fox Tale and Silver Fox Retreat, http://foxtale.org/index.html.

6. "Business: Furs from Fromms," *Time* (Monday, February 24, 1936), http://www.time.com/time/magazine/article/0,9171,755887,00.html.

7. Biennial report of the State Conservation Commission of Wisconsin for the fiscal years ending June 30, 1933, and June 30, 1934. Madison: 1934, 60, http://digital.library.wisc.edu/1711.dl/WI.RepConsCom34.

8. Wisconsin State Experimental Game and Fur Farm Guidebook, Wisconsin Conservation Department, 1935 (a hand-typed facsimile of guidebook text provided by Marv Kaukl).

9. Marv Kaukl, interview.

10. Ibid.

11. Ibid.

12. John Newhouse, "And Feat Impresses Seasoned Animal Men at Game Farm," *Wisconsin State Journal*, November 1954.

Chapter 23: "Le Portage" and the Fox-Wisconsin Waterway

1. Indian Agency House Website, www.agencyhouse.org/.

2. Nina Baym, "Juliette M. Kinzie's Wau-Bun: The 'Early Day' in the North-West," www.english.illinois.edu/-people-/emeritus/baym/essays/waubun.htm.

3. Margaret Beattie Bogue, "As She Knew Them, Juliette Kinzie and the Ho-Chunk, 1830–1833," *Wisconsin Magazine of History* (Winter 2001–2002): 48.
4. Ibid., 47.
5. Baym, "Juliette M. Kinzie's Wau-Bun."
6. Ina Curtis, *Early Days at the Fox-Wisconsin Portage* (self published, 1974), 28.
7. Baym, "Juliette M. Kinzie's Wau-Bun."
8. Mrs. John H. Kinzie, *Wau-Bun, The Early Day in the Northwest* (Menasha, WI: George Banta Publishing Company, 1930), 25–26.
9. Curtis, *Early Days at the Fox-Wisconsin Portage*.
10. Kinzie, *Wau-Bun, The Early Day in the Northwest*, 264.
11. Baym, "Juliette M. Kinzie's Wau-Bun."
12. Ibid.
13. Louise Phelps Kellogg, *The French Regime in Wisconsin and the Northwest* (Westminster, MD: Heritage Books, Inc., 2007), 191–194.
14. Jacques Marquette, The Mississippi Voyage of Jolliet and Marquette, 1673, American Journeys Collection, Wisconsin Historical Society, Document No. AJ-051, 235.
15. The Canadian Encyclopedia, "Fur Trade: Fur Trade in New France and Acadia," www.thecanadianencyclopedia.com/index.cfm?PgNm=TCE&Params=a1ARTA0003112.
16. Ibid.
17. Historical Sketch of Avon, Ohio, to 1974 by Taylor J Smith, www.centuryinter.net/tjs11/hist/hto74.htm
18. Indian Country Wisconsin Project of the Milwaukee Public Museum, www.mpm.edu/wirp/ICW-21.html.
19. Louise Phelps Kellogg, "The Fox Indians During the French Regime," Proceedings of the State Historical Society of Wisconsin at Its 55th annual meeting held November 7, 1907 (Madison: 1908), 142–188, online facsimile at www.wisconsinhistory.org/turningpoints/search.asp?id=1609
20. Ibid.
21. Ibid.
22. Ibid.
23. Indian Country Wisconsin Project of the Milwaukee Public Museum, www.mpm.edu/wirp/ICW-145.html.
24. Ibid.

25. W. A. Titus, "Historic Spots in Wisconsin," *The Wisconsin Magazine of History* (September 1926): 57.
26. Ibid., 59.
27. Ibid., 59–60.
28. Ibid., 60.

Chapter 24: Pioneer Bits and Pieces

1. "Went Fishing with Jackson," *Appleton Crescent*, December 1, 1906.
2. Ibid.
3. "Echoes of Old Madison," *Madison Capital Times*, January 29, 1923.
4. "Oldest Hunter Killed First Deer on Hotel Superior Site," *Superior Telegram*, November 13, 1914.
5. Ibid.
6. Ibid.
7. "Deer in Piles Like Cordwood No Uncommon Sight in Early Days," *Superior Telegram*, November 11, 1927.
8. Ibid.
9. "James D. Terry, Augusta, Comes to Bat with More Early Day Hunting Tales," *Eau Claire Telegram*, March 12, 1927.
10. Ibid.

Chapter 25: Charles Comiskey and the Northwoods

1. "Baseball as America," American Museum of Natural History, www.amnh.org/exhibitions/baseball/spirit/index.html.
2. G. W. Axelson, *"Commy": The Life Story of Charles A. Comiskey* (Chicago: Reilly and Lee, 1919), 268.
3. Ibid.
4. Ibid., 272.
5. "Comiskey at Mercer," *Rhinelander New North*, November 3, 1910.
6. "White Sox Take Annual Outing," *Rhinelander Daily News*, October 24, 1912.
7. Axelson, *Commy*, 272.
8. Ibid., 273.
9. Ibid.
10. "Comiskey Loses Another Moose," *Rhinelander New North*, September 28, 1916.

11. Ibid.
12. "Comiskey Host at Mercer Camp," *Rhinelander New North*, November 1, 1917.
13. Ibid.
14. "Improves Resort," *Rhinelander New North*, September 23, 1920.
15. "Comiskey Gets Deer," *Rhinelander New North*, December 2, 1920.
16. "Comiskey Dies at Dam Lake," *Rhinelander New North*, October 29, 1931.
17. Ibid.

Chapter 26: The Wisconsin White Pine That Built a New York University

1. Our Documents: 100 Milestone Documents from the National Archives, www.ourdocuments.gov/doc.php?flash=old&doc=33.
2. Ibid.
3. Cornell University 2001–2002 Financial Plan, http://dpb.cornell.edu/documents/1000046.pdf.
4. Ibid.
5. Paul Wallace Gates, *The Wisconsin Pine Lands of Cornell University, a Study in Land Policy and Absentee Ownership* (Ithaca, NY: Cornell University Press, 1943), 49.
6. Ibid., 90.
7. Ibid., 92.
8. Ibid., 102–103.
9. Ibid., 106.
10. Ibid., 208.
11. Ibid., 219.
12. Ibid., 225.
13. Ibid., 235.
14. Ibid., 232.
15. Ibid., 238.
16. Cornell University 2001–2002 Financial Plan.
17. Gates, *The Wisconsin Pine Lands of Cornell University*, 245.
18. Ibid., 250.

Index

Index

About the Author

Author photo by Jeff Koser

Robert C. Willging is a freelance outdoor and history writer whose work has appeared in *Deer & Deer Hunting, The Boundary Waters Journal, Wisconsin Outdoor Journal, Wisconsin Natural Resources, High Country News, Turkey Call, WildBird, The Trapper & Predator Caller, Fur-Fish-Game, Wisconsin Magazine of History, Wisconsin Outdoor News,* and other publications. His first book, *On the Hunt: The History of Deer Hunting in Wisconsin* was published by The Wisconsin Historical Society Press in 2008.

Willging holds a bachelor's degree in wildlife management from the University of Wisconsin—Stevens Point and a master's degree in wildlife sciences from New Mexico State University; he's worked as a wildlife biologist for the U. S. Department of Agriculture since 1987. An ardent sportsman, Willging frequently writes about Wisconsin's rich sporting past. He lives in Rhinelander with his wife and two children.